THE OPTION TRADER'S
GUIDE TO PROBABILITY,
VOLATILITY, AND TIMING

Founded in 1807, John Wiley & Sons is the oldest independent publishing company in the United States. With offices in North America, Europe, Australia, and Asia, Wiley is globally committed to developing and marketing print and electronic products and services for our customers' professional and personal knowledge and understanding.

The Wiley Trading Series features books by traders who have been able to work with the market's ever changing temperament and prosper—some by reinventing systems, others by getting back to basics. For the novice trader, professional, or somewhere in between, these books will provide the advice and strategies needed to prosper today and well into the future.

For a list of available titles, please visit our Web site at www.WileyFinance.com.

A Marketplace Book

THE OPTION TRADER'S GUIDE TO PROBABILITY, VOLATILITY, AND TIMING

Jay Kaeppel

John Wiley & Sons, Inc.

ISBN: 0-471-22619-X

10 9 8 7 6 5 4 3 2 1

In loving memory of Arthur H. Kaeppel

Contents

Contents

Foreword

Novice traders are attracted to the options market because of the degree of leverage and the vision of enhanced profitability it affords them. Options, however, are unlike any other exchange-traded product because of leverage, and more importantly, because of an attribute referred to as time decay. Unfortunately, traders learn the hard way that many factors besides calling the market direction correctly come into play in trading options. Most traders do not understand implied volatility, time decay, and out-of-the-money versus in-the-money options. Many do not have a working knowledge of which option strategies are best for any given situation, and they fail to understand just what the risk is before they make their trades.

Jay Kaeppel explains these issues in *The Option Trader's Guide to Probability, Volatility, and Timing*. Kaeppel covers the basics and then goes on to teach how to trade options. And he doesn't do it with get-rich-quick examples and hyperbole. He looks at the options market with a thorough analysis of both the risk and the profit potential of the various strategies, and he does so in a very readable fashion.

Kaeppel outlines the steps involved in becoming a successful trader. He explains the different strategies available and when to use each one. He shows how to accurately assess volatility and from there, how to profit by disparities in the implied volatilities of different options. His strategies include guidelines for determining when to buy undervalued options and when to sell overvalued options. Finally, Kaeppel teaches when to take a profit, and most importantly, when to cut losses and move on to the next trade.

The key value of this book is its objectivity and its details. The guidelines are clear and objective, not a collection of anecdotal examples that have happened once or twice. Save yourself some money and benefit from this money manager's experience and wisdom if you want to profit in the options market.

THOM HARTLE
2001

Thom Hartle (www.thomhartle.com) is a trader and educator working with private trades, as well as a contributing editor for *Active Trader Magazine.*

Chapter 1

INTRODUCTION

Who Can Benefit from This Book

This book is written for people who fall into one of two categories:

1. Those who are new to option trading and looking for a good place to start
2. Those who have traded options in the past and did not achieve the type of success they had hoped to

Option trading enjoyed explosive growth during the late 1990s and into the start of the new millennium, particularly among individuals. Traders whose bankrolls were fattened by the great bull market in stocks fueled part of this growth. Having enjoyed great success in the stock market, many people decided to try to increase their gains by accessing the leverage associated with options. Along the way computers got faster and more powerful, technology advanced rapidly, and markets traded with greater volume and volatility than ever before. Yet there is much about option trading that is no different than it ever was. Through all the years and all the growth and changes, critical elements remain that traders must understand and apply consistently if they hope to succeed in the long run. The purpose of this book is to illuminate these concepts and show how to apply them successfully in real-world trading.

What Sets This Book Apart

The primary focus of this book is not to teach you *about* options, but rather to teach you how to successfully *trade* options. Having a textbook understanding of any topic is not the same thing as applying that knowledge in the real world. This book is intended to give new traders and returnees to the options market an understanding of what it takes to succeed, as well as a set of guidelines to apply in the real world of trading. Most of all, it is intended to make traders aware of the sobering realities of option trading, including the financial risks involved. No attempt is made to candy-coat the fact that garnering consistent profits in the options market over a long period is a difficult goal to achieve.

Can Options Really Be Simplified?

Options are by nature fairly complex. Not only are there many trading strategies to consider, there also are many different factors that apply to trade selection and position management. To complicate things even further, some factors matter a lot with certain strategies and not as much with others. Nevertheless, despite the inherent complexities, it is possible to gain an understanding of these key factors without a Ph.D. in finance. This book will introduce you to the most important basic concepts in option trading and illustrate why an understanding of these concepts is critical to your long-term success. In the later chapters of this book, the concepts are applied to a number of different trading strategies to show you how to get the most out of each situation.

What This Book Provides

A careful reading of the material in this book will give you the following:

- An introduction to the most valuable uses of options
- Basic option terminology

- Explanations of the most important concepts in option trading
- Explanations of the most useful trading strategies available
- The conditions to look for when deciding which strategy to employ
- Objective guidelines for employing each strategy
- Objective guidelines for exiting a trade at a loss
- Objective guidelines for exiting a trade at a profit

Overview of Option Trading

Most option traders use options simply as a tool to leverage their market-timing decisions. They buy call options when they think an advance is imminent and they buy put options when they think a decline is forthcoming. Unfortunately, because buying calls and puts involves buying a *wasting asset*, in most cases this approach ends up being unprofitable. It is estimated that 90% or more of people who trade options lose money in the long run. If this is true, it is a staggering number. However, a high failure rate is not all that surprising when you consider the complexity involved in trading options and the fact that most option traders do not take the time to develop a well-thought-out plan before they begin trading. In addition, many traders are poorly prepared to deal with the emotional aspects of trading.

It is vitally important to your long-term success that you use a structured approach to trading.

This is not to imply that your trading approach must be completely systematic. What it means is that you must establish and follow some reasonably well-thought-out guidelines if you hope to achieve consistent success. Markets can turn on a dime. If you do not have a well-thought-out trading plan, you will find yourself chasing each twist and turn of the market. In addition, if you do not develop the discipline to follow your trading plan, the odds are overwhelming that you will join the 90% of traders who lose money.

To go one step further, not only should you have a plan before you start trading, you must plan each option trade in terms of how you will manage each position once you have entered into it. There is no one best trading strategy; each one has strengths and weaknesses. By examining the best-case and worst-case scenarios for each trade, you can establish objective criteria for when to exit each trade, whether you are taking a profit or cutting a loss.

Too many traders enter the markets on a whim, without carefully considering either

- The likelihood that they will be successful in the long run
- The potential pitfalls they may encounter and what they can do to avoid them

The material in this book is written to help you as a trader by providing a specific trading plan, using well-thought-out and market-tested criteria for entering and exiting each trade. It is also intended to help you hone your ability to think like a trader by walking you through example trades to let you develop a feel for the process of deciding on

- Strategy selection
- Individual trade selection
- Position-management guidelines

Each strategy chapter in this book (Chapters 12 through 19) delineates a specific set of rules for each strategy. Be assured that there is no intent to convince you that this is the only way to use a given strategy. The underlying point is my belief that traders are better off in the long run if they adopt one approach they are comfortable with for a given strategy than if they make it up as they go along, using one approach one time and a different approach the next time.

The Benefits of an Objective Approach

Traders gain a psychological benefit from doing their best thinking up front and building a well-thought-out trading plan. After that, they are simply following the rules. One thing to remember is that your trading plan will not always maximize your profit on each and every trade. This is simply a reality of trading. The benefits of using an objective approach to option trading include these:

- Eliminating emotional decision making
- Relieving the psychological burden of being right or wrong in each situation
- Doing your best thinking up front and then trusting in your plan, rather than having to make subjective decisions in the heat of battle

Constructing a well-thought-out trading plan is a crucial step toward consistent trading success. A trading plan relieves a great deal of the emotional pressure that traders feel when they rely on gut instinct and hunches to trade. Too many traders assume that they will know the right thing to do when the time arrives. In reality, more often than not this turns out to be exactly the opposite of what actually occurs. In a bad situation, with real money on the line, unprepared traders make emotional decisions based solely on fear or greed. Very often these are decisions that they would never make if they were thinking rationally.

The good news about developing a trading plan is that a well-thought-out plan can serve as a road map to trading profits by keeping you from overreacting to every bend in the road. The bad news is that no approach to trading is perfect. There are no magic formulas or holy grail for trading.

The surest way to succeed as a trader is to develop a trading approach that has a realistic probability of making money in the long run and then to stick to your plan.

Here are the key steps in this process.

1. Identify criteria that give you the greatest probability of success in the long run.
2. Develop confidence in the approach you are using. Confidence comes from establishing criteria that cover all the following bases:

- When to use a particular strategy
- When to enter a trade
- When to exit a trade at a profit
- When to exit a trade at a loss

3. Develop the discipline to stick to your approach even when things are not going well. This comes from having the confidence developed in Step 2.

Once you reach this point, your trading process becomes second nature. Through good times and bad you continue to trade consistently, confident that in the long run you will come out ahead. This is a trait of all successful traders.

Understanding Risk by Using Risk Curves

A *risk curve* is a graph that depicts the profit or loss characteristics for a given option trade. Analyzing a risk curve allows a trader to visualize the market action needed to make money on that particular trade. Such a graph is also useful in assessing

- Break-even points and probability of profit
- Maximum risk
- Profit potential

Additionally, two or more risk curves can be analyzed to determine which trade offers the reward-to-risk characteristics a trader deems most attractive.

More than anything, a risk curve is a *forest-from-the-trees* tool. For any option trade, it does not really matter in the end what the position is—whether it is long a call, long a spread, short a spread, or any other combination. In the final analysis the only questions that matter are these:

- What has to happen in order for me to make money on this trade?
- What is my worst-case scenario?

A risk curve allows you to visualize the answer to these all-important questions. Risk curves are used throughout this book

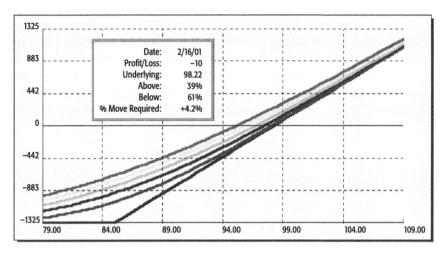

Date:	2/16/01
Profit/Loss:	−10
Underlying:	98.22
Above:	39%
Below:	61%
% Move Required:	+4.2%

Figure 1.1 Risk curves for IBM February 85 call option (from 79 to 109).

to depict the profit and loss characteristics of various trades. Let's look at an example to help you understand what these graphs show and why the information they contain is so important.

Figure 1.1 shows risk curves for a position that involves buying the IBM February 85 call option on January 5 at a price of 13.25 ($1325). A range of prices for the stock is listed along the bottom of the graph, with the current price of 94 in the middle. The graph shows the profitability of this trade based on an underlying stock price ranging from 79 to 104. The actual expected dollar profit or loss is listed on the left side of the graph.

Each curve on the graph displays the expected profit or loss at a given stock price as of a given date. This trade was initiated on January 5. The top curve shows the expected return as of January 12, the next curve as of January 19, then January 26, February 2, February 9, and finally, the date of the February option expiration, which is February 16. Much useful information may be gleaned from this graph.

The Effect of Time Decay

The first thing to note is the effect of time decay. As we discuss in detail in Chapter 5, *time decay* refers to the erosion of an option price as time passes and option expiration draws nearer. The obvious implication from this graph is that the buyer of this option stands to earn a greater profit if the price of the stock rises sooner rather than later. As the price of the option erodes slightly with each passing day due to time decay, a larger price move by the underlying security is required to offset this loss.

Break-Even Analysis and Probability of Profit

The lowest curve on the graph in Figure 1.1 displays the expected profit or loss if the option is held until expiration. Although many options are exited before expiration, it is often helpful to know where a trade is going to end up eventually if the trader does nothing before expiration. In this case the break-even point is 98.25 (which equals the strike price of 85 plus the price paid for the option of 13.25). Based on the volatility of IBM stock when this trade is entered, there is a 39% probability that IBM will rise from 94 to 98.25 or higher by the time of February option expiration. This probability value is most useful when compared to the probability value for another potential trade. By comparing two or more trades, a trader can determine which is most likely to generate a profit.

Maximum Risk

Whenever you buy an option, your risk is limited to whatever price you paid to buy the option. In this example the buyer paid $1325 to buy the option. You can see by the lowest curve on the graph in Figure 1.1 that the maximum loss will occur if the stock is trading at 80 or lower at the time of option expiration. In other words, even if IBM stock fell to 70 or 60 or 50 or less, the option buyer's loss in this example would never exceed $1325. This illustrates the *limited risk* feature associated with buying options.

Profit Potential

In addition to limited risk, buying an option gives a trader unlimited profit potential. Figure 1.2 shows the same trade as that

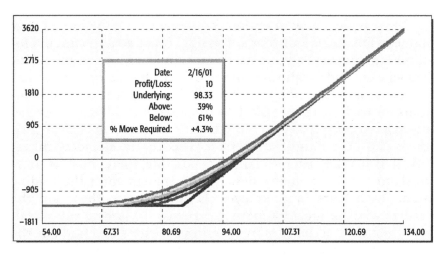

Figure 1.2 Risk curves for IBM February 85 call option (from 54 to 134).

in Fugure 1.1. The only difference is that the price range along the bottom of the graph has been expanded from 15 points above and below the current price of the stock to 40 points above and below the current price of the stock. This range is expanded to illustrate the profit potential available if IBM makes a substantial move in price.

As you can see, if IBM were to rally 40 points by option expiration, the buyer of this option could earn a profit of $3620 on a $1325 investment. Although the probability of this happening may be low, it represents a return of 173% and vividly illustrates the huge profit potential of buying options.

Asking the Right Question

Too many traders focus on probability or profit potential and completely ignore risk.

When assessing the prospects for any given trade, the right question is not "How much can I make?" The right question is "What is my worst-case scenario and how do I mitigate this risk?" According to an old adage in trade, "As long as you minimize losses, profits will take care of themselves."

Most traders new to options are attracted by the lure of easy money. This is not all that surprising. Most advertisements for option trading play on traders' desire to make a lot of money fast. Traders read ads claiming that they can double or triple their money in a matter of a few short weeks, pinpoint tops and bottoms, or trade without risk. It is not as though all traders are so naïve as to completely buy into this type of hype, but over time there can be a cumulative effect. Eventually a trader thinks, "Well, if so many people claim it is possible, there must be some truth to it." Thus, many new option traders enter the trading arena with stars in their eyes. Unfortunately, these are the traders who are most likely to experience the jarring jolt of reality when they actually start entering positions and find out the real secret of trading.

The real secret of trading is simply that there is no easy money to be made in trading!

Bad things happen even to the very best traders:

- Markets often reverse unexpectedly or gap sharply in the wrong direction.
- Markets can be choppy and trendless for frustratingly long periods.
- Buy orders get filled at the high of the day.
- Sell orders get filled at the low of the day.
- If you increase your trading size after a string of winners, the next trade will be a big loser.
- If you stop trading after a string of losers, the next trade you don't take will be a big winner.

It is how one reacts to unpleasant experiences that separates the long-term winners from the 90% of traders who lose money.

One of the keys to trading success is to avoid the big hit. One devastating loss can wipe out a significant portion of your trading capital, and the psychological damage can be irreparable, often rendering a trader incapable of functioning rationally on future trades. You are much more likely to be successful if you recognize, acknowledge, and plan out how you will deal with the worst-case scenario in each instance than you are if you believe blindly that whatever it is you are doing will somehow prevail, even in the face of extremely adverse conditions.

If you look at each trade you make and identify the worst-case scenario that might result, you can develop an objective plan in advance for dealing with that possibility. This allows you to build a safety net, which can keep you from suffering the devastating big hit.

Before you worry about making big money, you must insulate yourself from the danger of losing big money. The only way to do this is to address risk before reward.

Analyzing Risk: What Separates the Winners from the Losers

One key to *making* money is to avoid *losing* money!
To avoid losing money you must

• Acknowledge the downside risk of any trade
• Develop a contingency plan to deal with this risk

The one thing you cannot do is pretend that risk doesn't exist!

If you asked traders who have enjoyed long-term success for the key to their success, the vast majority of them would tell you it was

• Cutting losses
• Controlling risk

Everybody gets into trading to make money. It is interesting that those who end up being most successful in this endeavor often spend more time focusing on not losing money than they do on making money.

One of the keys to option trading success is understanding the risks involved in any trade and then planning to minimize these risks.

When traders learn about option-trading strategies, they often don't receive enough information to fully understand the risks involved. In the following pages are two case studies of trades that, on the surface, could be touted by market gurus as high-probability, sure-thing, you-can't-lose trades. In fact, most discussions of these strategies fail to answer the right question— "What is my risk on this trade?"

Novice traders are quick to latch onto ideas that promise the potential for huge profits. Unfortunately, too many traders are subconsciously content as long as they believe they have a chance to make a lot of money, regardless of the reality of the situation. Whether the trades actually work out or not ends up being a secondary consideration. Until the mounting losses become too great, they continue to hope that the next trade will be the big one.

Too often, traders are so focused on the idea of making a lot of money that they fail to account for or even acknowledge the risks involved in the trades they make. This is the road to trading failure.

Case 1: Ratio Spread

The trade presented in Figure 1.3 looks extremely enticing. The strategy used in this trade is referred to as a *ratio spread*. This trade uses options on Coffee futures and involves buying one call option with a strike price of 700 and simultaneously selling two further-out-of-the-money options with a strike price of 750. The risk curve shows the profit or loss that a trader holding this position would experience if the trade were held until

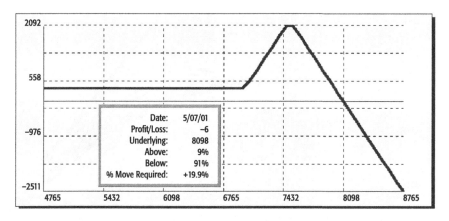

Figure 1.3 Risk curve for Coffee call ratio spread at expiration.

option expiration. The expected dollar profit or loss is listed down the left side of the graph, and a range of underlying prices are listed across the bottom of the graph.

If the trade is held until option expiration, there is

- *A 91% probability of profit.* In other words, with Coffee trading at 6765 when the trade is entered, there is a 91% probability that Coffee will be trading below the break-even price of 8098 at the time of option expiration.
- *Unlimited risk if Coffee is above 8098.* However, when the trade is entered, there is only a 9% probability of Coffee rising from 6765 to 8098 or higher by the time of option expiration.
- A maximum profit potential of $2032.
- A guaranteed profit if Coffee stays at 7000 or below.

This trade inarguably offers some great potential benefits. However, looking at this trade only at expiration fails to answer the most important questions. The most important questions to answer before entering any trade are not "How much can I make?" or "What is the probability that I will profit?" The questions you need to answer are "How bad can things get?" and "What do I plan to do about it?"

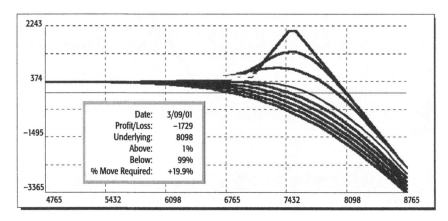

Figure 1.4 Risk curves for Coffee call ratio spread leading up to expiration.

As you will see in Figure 1.4, to answer these questions you have to look at what could happen to this trade before expiration.

Call ratio spread:

- Long 1 June 700 call at 350.
- Short 2 June 750 calls at 230.
- 67 days to expiration.
- Initial credit = $413.
- As long as Coffee is below 8098 at option expiration, this trade is profitable.
- A 91% probability of profit.
- Profit potential of $2092.
- Complete downside protection.

Sounds great! But the risk curves in Figure 1.4 paint a much more illuminating picture of the risks involved with this trade than does the graph in Figure 1.3. Each of the curves on the graph depict the expected profit or loss as of a different date based on the price of Coffee at that time. A range of Coffee prices is listed along the bottom of the graph.

By looking at the risk curves on several dates leading up to expiration, we get a more realistic picture of the risk involved. The real risk in this trade is not that Coffee will be trading above 8098 at the time of option expiration. The real risk in this trade is that Coffee prices will experience a sustained move upward immediately after the trade is entered. If Coffee rallies sooner rather than later, traders may be holding a trade with a large open loss. Although the probability of this happening may be low, when you consider that Coffee once opened 3000 points higher, you can begin to appreciate the need to acknowledge that such a thing could happen and the potential impact that such a move could have on this trade. Therefore, you need to know how such a move would affect your position to ensure that you could weather the worst-case scenario.

The key is not in figuring out what to do once the worst-case scenario unfolds. The key is advance planning to avoid getting into such a situation in the first place.

This type of planning would be impossible if you looked only at the risk curve at expiration, which is what the graph in Figure 1.3 shows. Unfortunately, the graph showing how the trade would work out if it were held until expiration is the one that usually shows up when option-trading strategies are discussed. As you can see in Figure 1.4, the single risk curve drawn at expiration does not tell the full story.

It is impossible to overemphasize the importance of recognizing the risks that exist for any given trade and planning in advance to minimize risk should the worst-case scenario unfold, rather than waiting for the worst to happen and then trying to figure out how to save your skin!

There is a 91% probability of profit if the position is held to expiration; however,

- If Coffee rallies sharply before expiration, large unlimited losses can occur!
- Maximum profit potential of $2092 occurs only if Coffee closes exactly at 7500 at expiration!

Case 2: Synthetic Long Futures Position

The trade presented in Figure 1.5 appears to be close to a sure thing. The strategy used in this example is referred to as a *synthetic long futures position*. The trade is established by buying an out-of-the-money call and simultaneously writing an out-of-the-money put. The risk curve depicts the profit or loss for a trader holding this position if the trade is held until option expiration. The expected dollar profit or loss is listed down the left side of the graph, and a range of underlying futures prices are listed across the bottom of the graph.

If this trade is held until expiration,

- There is an 80% probability of profit. In other words, with S&P 500 futures trading at 1239 as the trade is entered, there is an 80% probability that S&P 500 futures will be trading above the break-even price of 1170 at the time of option expiration.

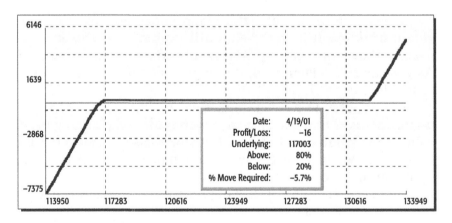

Figure 1.5   Risk curve for S&P synthetic futures at expiration.

- There is unlimited risk if the S&P 500 falls below 1170. However, when this trade is entered there is only a 20% probability of the S&P 500 declining from 1239 to 1170 or lower by the time of option expiration.
- This trade has unlimited upside potential.

Unfortunately, just as in Case 1, looking at this trade only at expiration fails to answer the most important question about risk. Remember, the questions you need to answer are "How bad can things get?" and "What do I plan to do about it?" To answer these questions, you must again look at what could happen to this trade before expiration (see Figure 1.6).

Synthetic futures: long a call, short a put

- Long 1 Apr 1320 call at 1730.
- Short 1 Apr 1175 put at 1830.
- As long as S&P is above 1170 at option expiration, this trade is profitable.
- An 80% probability of profit.
- Unlimited profit potential.

Sounds like a sure thing! But as with the Coffee trade in Case 1, the risk curves in Figure 1.6 paint a much more illumi-

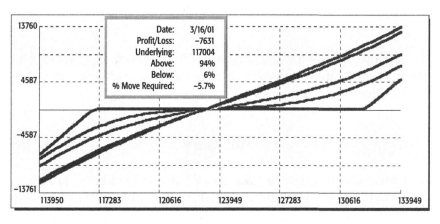

Figure 1.6 Risk curves for S&P synthetic futures leading up to expiration.

nating picture of the risks involved with this trade than does the graph in Figure 1.5. By looking at the risk curves on several dates before expiration, we get a more realistic picture of the risk involved.

The real risk in this trade is not that the S&P will fall below 1170 at expiration. The real risk is that the S&P will decline sharply before expiration. If the S&P falls sooner than later, the trader may be holding a large open loss. The key is not figuring out what to do once this occurs; the key is to plan in order to avoid getting into such a situation in the first place. This type of planning would be impossible if you looked only at the risk curve at expiration, which was shown in the graph in Figure 1.5. Unfortunately, the graph showing how the trade would work out if it were held until expiration is the one that usually shows up when various option-trading strategies are discussed. As you can see in Figure 1.6, the single profit/loss line drawn at expiration does not tell the full story.

NOTE

The purpose of this example is not to imply that synthetic futures are a bad idea nor that option educational materials are purposefully misleading when all they include is a profit/loss graph as of option expiration. The purpose is simply to illustrate the importance of identifying and planning for the risks involved with any trade. It is impossible to state definitively that this is a good trade or a bad trade—that is up to each trader to determine.

As long as the S&P is above 1170 at option expiration, this trade is profitable; however, if S&P falls sooner than later, unlimited losses can occur!

Summary

The primary message to take away from this chapter is simply that options differ in many ways from other forms of investment. When you buy a stock or a futures contract, you either make a point for each point it rises in price, or you lose a point for each point it declines. With options it is not always so straightforward.

You should also prepare yourself to focus on the key elements that must be understood and applied to achieve success in option trading.

Chapter 2

THE BASICS OF OPTIONS

Before one can hope to succeed in any field of endeavor, one must have a firm grasp of the fundamental concepts. It is no different in the field of option trading. Anyone can get lucky on a trade now and then, but a solid understanding of the basics is required to achieve consistent long-term success. Option trading has a vocabulary all its own. In this chapter you will learn many common and essential terms.

When you buy or sell short a stock or a futures contract, the results you can expect are fairly straightforward. If you buy 100 shares of stock and that stock goes up 5 points, you will make $500. If it goes down 5 points, you will lose $500. With options, these simple parameters do not apply. Depending on the option or options you choose to buy or write, your expected return and the amount of risk you are exposed to can vary greatly. Before delving into these possibilities, let's define some important option terms.

Option Definitions

Call option.   A call buyer pays a premium to the option writer, which gives the option buyer the right, within a specified period, to buy 100 shares of stock (or one futures contract) at a specified price (known as the *strike price*), no matter how high the stock price may rise. For example, say a trader buys a call option with a strike price of 50. The stock then rises to 100. By virtue of holding a call option with a strike price of 50, the trader can *exercise* the option and buy 100 shares of stock at a price of 50 a share.

Put option.   A put buyer pays a premium to the option writer, which gives the option buyer the right, within a specified period, to sell 100 shares of stock (or one futures contract) at a specific price, no matter how low the stock price may fall. For example, say a trader buys a put option with a strike price of 50. The stock then falls to 10. Because the trader holds a put option with a strike price of 50, the trader can exercise the option and sell 100 shares of stock at 50.

Underlying.   In the world of options, the word *underlying* refers to the security on which a given option is based. For example, IBM is the underlying security for all IBM options. In futures markets, Soybean futures are the underlying for all Soybean options.

Option buyer.   The person who buys an option.

Option writer.   The person who writes an option.

Option premium.   The price of an option contract. Stock options are for 100 shares, so a stock option that is quoted at a price of $5 (or 5), represents an *option premium* of $500 (100 × $5). The option premium is the amount that the option buyer pays to the option writer. It also represents the total amount of risk assumed by the buyer of the option and the maximum amount of profit that can be obtained by the writer of the option.

Strike price or exercise price.   The strike price is the price at which an option can be exercised, that is, the price per share that the buyer of a call option must pay to buy the stock if the buyer chooses to exercise his or her option. Option exchanges designate the available strike prices for each listed security. For most stocks the default range between strike prices is 5 points (e.g., 25, 30, 35, 40). Many stocks also offer strike prices at 2.5-point increments below 30 (e.g., 2.5, 7.5, 12.5, 17.5, 22.5, 27.5). If a stock or stock index reaches a price above 200, the options often trade only in increments of 10 points or more (e.g., 250,

260, 270, 280). Strike prices for options on futures are set by the exchange and vary from commodity to commodity.

Expiration date. The date after which an option is void and ceases to exist is its expiration date. For U.S. stock options, the expiration date is the third Friday of the expiration month. In other words, June options expire on the third Friday in June, July options expire on the third Friday in July, and so on. For futures options, the expiration months and expiration dates can vary and are set by the exchange on which a given series of options is traded.

Expiration cycle. For U.S. stock options, the exchange on which the options are traded designates a particular *expiration cycle*—either a January cycle, February cycle, March cycle, or all months. The expiration months for the options on a given stock are determined by the expiration cycle assigned to that stock.

Theoretical price or fair value. The price at which a given option is considered fairly valued based on a combination of variables used in a standard option pricing model is called the option's fair value (see Chapter 4 for more details on option pricing).

In-the-money option. A call option is in the money if its strike price is *less* than the current market price of the underlying. A put option is in the money if its strike price is *higher* than the current market price of the underlying.

A call option with a strike price of 50 is considered in the money as long as the price of the stock is greater than 50. A put option with a strike price of 50 is considered in the money as long as the price of the stock is less than 50.

Out-of-the-money option. An option that currently has no intrinsic value is an out-of-the-money option. A call option is out of the money if its exercise price is *higher* than the current market price of the underlying. A put option is out of the-money if its exercise price is *lower* than the current price of the underlying.

A call option with a strike price of 50 is considered out of the money as long as the price of the stock is less than 50. A put option with a strike price of 50 is considered out of the money as long as the price of the stock is greater than 50.

At-the-money option.   For any security, the option whose strike price is currently closest to the actual price of the underlying security is generally referred to as the at-the-money strike. Please note that, technically speaking, the at-the-money option is usually slightly in or out of the money. For example, if a stock is trading at a price of 96, the 95 call and the 95 put options are considered the at-the-money strikes, even though the call option is 1 point in the money and the put is 1 point out of the money.

Intrinsic value.   The amount by which an option is in the money is its intrinsic value. An out-of-the-money option has no intrinsic value. If a call option has a strike price of 50 and the underlying stock is trading at 55, the 50 call option has 5 points of intrinsic value. If a put option has a strike price of 50 and the underlying stock is trading at 45, the 50 put option has 5 points of intrinsic value.

Extrinsic value (or time premium).   The price of an option less its intrinsic value is its extrinsic value. The entire premium of an out-of-the-money option consists of extrinsic value, or time premium. *Time premium* is essentially the amount an option buyer pays to the option seller (above and beyond the intrinsic value of the option) to induce the seller to enter into the trade. All options lose the entire time premium at expiration, a phenomenon referred to as *time decay* (see Chapter 5).

Long.   A long position results from the purchase of an option contract.

Short.   A short position results from the short sale of an option contract, also known as *writing a contract.*

Buy premium or long premium.   A buy premium results when you enter into a position where you are paying more money for the option you buy than you take in for any option you may write.

Sell premium or short premium.   A sell premium results from entering into a position where you are taking in more money for the option you buy than you pay out for any option you may write.

Naked option. Buying an option of a single strike price is considered a naked long option. Writing an option of a single strike price is considered a naked short position. The buyer of the IBM 95 call is holding a long naked option. The writer of the IBM 95 call is holding a short naked option.

Spread. A spread position involves buying or writing options of different strike prices or different expiration months. A trader who buys the IBM 95 call and simultaneously writes the IBM 100 call has entered into a spread position.

Historic volatility. A value calculated based on the price fluctuations of the underlying security is the stock's historic volatility. This value represents an estimate of how far the underlying security is likely to fluctuate in price over the ensuing 12-month period. A stock with a historic volatility of 20% would be expected to fluctuate plus or minus 20% from its current price over the ensuing 12 months.

Implied option volatility. The implied option volatility is the value that must be plugged into an option pricing model to cause the model to arrive at the current market price as an output, given the other known variables (see Chapter 4, Option Pricing, and Chapter 6, Volatility). It may also be referred to as option volatility and implied volatility.

Overvalued option. An option is considered overvalued if market price is greater than the theoretical price generated for that option by an option pricing model.

Undervalued option. An option is considered undervalued if its market price is less than the theoretical price generated for that option by an option pricing model.

Expensive option. An option can be considered expensive if implied volatility is high relative to the historic range of implied volatility for options on the underlying security (see Chapter 6).

Inexpensive option. An option can be considered inexpensive or cheap if its implied volatility is low relative to the historic range of implied volatility for options on the underlying security (see Chapter 6).

Options on a Specific Security

On January 5, IBM closed at a price of 94. Table 2.1 shows most of the available call and put options for IBM at that time. The strike prices—in this case, ranging from 70 to 120—are listed down the left side of each grid. The available expiration months and the number of days left until expiration for each available month is listed across the top of each grid.

Table 2.1 shows the latest market price for each option. For example, the February 95 call option has 42 days left until expiration and is currently trading at a price of 6.88. The April 90 put has 106 days left until expiration and is trading at a price of 7.88.

By examining the price grid you can see that as the strike prices get higher, call prices decrease and put prices increase. This happens because at each successively higher strike price there is less intrinsic value in each call option price and more intrinsic value in each put option price. As strike prices go lower, call prices increase and put prices decrease. This happens because at each successively lower strike price there is more intrinsic value in each call option price and less intrinsic value in each put option price.

Table 2.1	Market Price of IBM Options on January 5 (Stock Price = 94)

		Calls						Puts			
		JAN 14	FEB 42	APR 106	JUL 197			JAN 14	FEB 42	APR 106	JUL 197
70	Market	24.25	25.00	26.88	28.88	70	Market	.44	1.00	2.12	3.38
75	Market	19.75	20.50	22.88	2.25	75	Market	.62	1.44	2.88	4.38
80	Market	15.25	16.50	19.75	21.50	80	Market	1.38	2.38	4.25	5.62
85	Market	11.12	13.00	15.75	18.50	85	Market	2.06	3.62	5.88	7.38
90	Market	7.88	9.50	13.12	15.75	90	Market	3.50	5.12	7.88	9.88
95	Market	4.50	6.88	10.12	13.25	95	Market	5.25	7.62	10.12	12.00
100	Market	2.38	4.75	8.00	10.88	100	Market	8.12	10.12	12.50	14.38
105	Market	1.31	3.00	6.12	8.88	105	Market	12.50	13.38	16.25	17.38
110	Market	.62	2.00	4.88	7.50	110	Market	17.00	17.75	19.12	20.62
115	Market	.31	1.25	3.50	6.12	115	Market	21.62	21.38	23.00	24.38
120	Market	.12	.56	2.62	4.75	120	Market	25.75	25.88	27.00	28.25

Call Options

Table 2.1 and Figures 2.1 through 2.3 depict the risk curves at expiration for 3 separate IBM call options: the deep-in-the-money 80 call, the at-the-money 95 call, and the far-out-of-the-money 115 call.

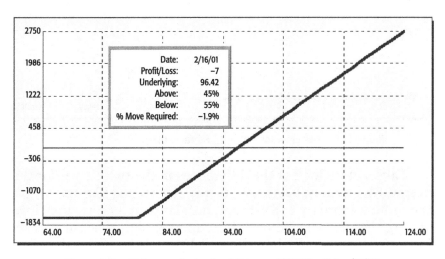

Figure 2.1   Risk curve for buying 1 February IBM 80 call for $1650.

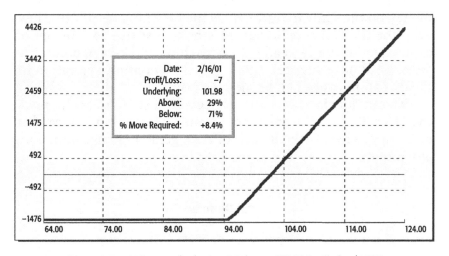

Figure 2.2   Risk curve for buying 2 February IBM 95 calls for $1375.

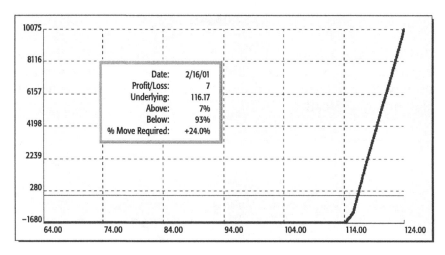

Figure 2.3   Risk curve for buying 13 February IBM 115 calls for $1625.

Take a close look at the differences in the risk curves for the deep-in-the-money February 80 call option and the far-out-of-the-money February 115 call option. Many traders are lured into buying the inexpensive out-of-the-money option because of its low price (a trader can buy thirteen 115 calls for about the same cost as one 80 call, which to some traders represents a deal they just can't pass up). In fact, if IBM makes a big jump in price, the buyer of the 115 calls stands to make almost four times as much money on the same investment as the buyer of one 80 call. However, the tradeoff here is that the stock must rise 24% by option expiration for the 115 call just to reach its break-even point. The stock need only advance 1.9% or more by option expiration for the 80 call to exceed its break-even point.

In sum, for the trader who expects IBM stock to rise in price, the 115 call offers the greater opportunity for making a great deal of money, whereas the 80 call offers a greater chance of making any money.

Put Options

Figures 2.4 through 2.6 depict the risk curves for three separate IBM put options: the far-out-of-the-money 80 put, the at-the-money 95 put, and the deep-in-the-money 115 put.

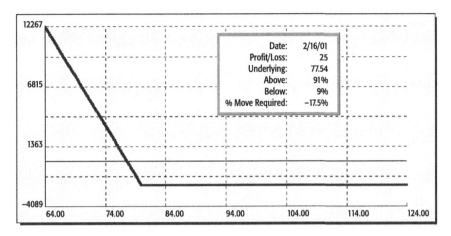

Date:	2/16/01
Profit/Loss:	25
Underlying:	77.54
Above:	91%
Below:	9%
% Move Required:	−17.5%

Figure 2.4   Buy 9 February IBM 80 puts for $2138.

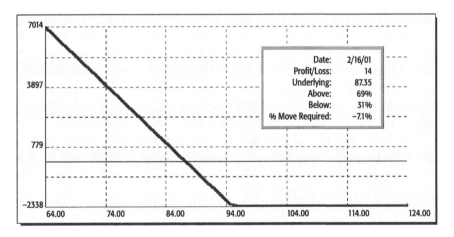

Date:	2/16/01
Profit/Loss:	14
Underlying:	87.35
Above:	69%
Below:	31%
% Move Required:	−7.1%

Figure 2.5   Buy 3 February IBM 95 puts for $2288.

Take a close look at the differences in the risk curves for the far-out-of-the-money February 80 put option and the deep-in-the-money February 115 put option. Many traders are lured into buying the inexpensive out-of-the-money option because of its low price (a trader can buy nine 80 puts for the about the same cost as one 115 put, which to some traders represents a deal they

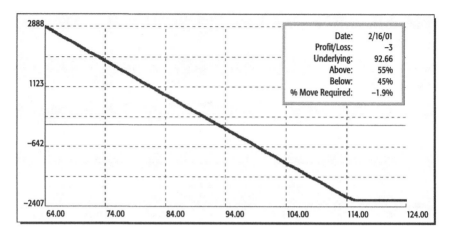

Date:	2/16/01
Profit/Loss:	–3
Underlying:	92.66
Above:	55%
Below:	45%
% Move Required:	–1.9%

Figure 2.6   Buy 1 February IBM 115 put for $2138.

just can't pass up). In fact, if IBM stock declines dramatically, the buyer of the 80 put stands to make more than four times as much money on the same investment as the buyer of one 115 put. However, the tradeoff here is that the stock must decline –17.5% by option expiration for the 80 put to reach its break-even point. The stock need only decline –1.9% or more by option expiration for the 115 put to exceed its break-even point.

In sum, for the trader who truly expects IBM stock to fall sharply in price, the 80 put offers the greater opportunity for making lots of money, whereas the 115 put offers a greater chance of making any money.

Intrinsic Value versus Extrinsic Value

Table 2.2 shows the current price for several IBM call options and breaks the current price down into intrinsic value and extrinsic value. Column 1 shows the option's strike price, Column 2 shows the actual price of the option, Column 3 shows the amount of intrinsic value built into the price of the option, and Column 4 shows the amount of extrinsic value—or time premium—built into the current option price. These figures are

Table 2.2   Intrinsic and Extrinsic Value

February Option	Call Price	Intrinsic Value	Time Premium	Price at Expiration*
85 call	13.00	9.00	4.00	9.00
90 call	9.50	4.00	5.50	4.00
95 call	6.88	0.00	6.88	0.00

*If IBM is trading at a price of 94 at the time of expiration.

based on IBM trading at 94 on January 5. With 42 days left until February option expiration,

- 31% of the price of the 85 call is made up of the time premium (4.00 of time premium divided by the 13.00 option price)
- 81% of the price of the 90 call is made up of the time premium (5.50 of time premium divided by the 9.50 option price)
- 100% of the price of the 95 call is made up of the time premium (6.88 of time premium divided by the 6.88 option price)

The last column shows how much the option will be worth if IBM is still trading at 94 at the time of option expiration. Notice that the price at expiration is exactly equal to the intrinsic value.

A beginning trader might wonder, "Why is there time premium in the price of each option? How come options don't just trade for their intrinsic value, since that is the only real value they have?" The answer is that time premium can be thought of as a premium paid to the option writer in order to induce him or her to assume the risk of writing an option, which can expose the option writer to unlimited risk. Similarly, if the underlying security happens to be extremely volatile, the option writer is likely to demand more of a premium than if volatility is low. This is roughly equivalent to an insurance company charging a higher premium to insure a high-risk driver. In other words, to assume the unlimited risk associated with writing options in a volatile market, the option writer demands more premium in order to compensate for this risk. This is discussed in more detail in Chapters 4 through 6.

In-the-Money versus Out-of-the-Money Options

Which option a trader chooses to purchase has a significant impact on the cost of entry, the profit potential, and the probability of profit. Consider the following example. On January 5, a trader with $3000 to invest expects IBM to rise before the February option expiration. She considers the following choices:

- Buy 3 February 90 calls at 9.88 for $2962.
- Buy 4 February 95 calls at 7.12 for $2850.
- Buy 6 February 100 calls at 4.88 for $2925.

What are the implications for each choice? The best way to assess the relative advantages and disadvantages is to examine the risk curves for each potential trade.

Figures 2.7 through 2.9 depict the risk curves for the three options closest to the money—the 90, 95, and 100 strike prices—with IBM trading at a price of 94.

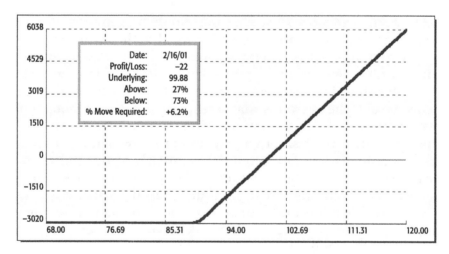

Figure 2.7   Risk curve for buying 3 February 90 calls at 9.88.

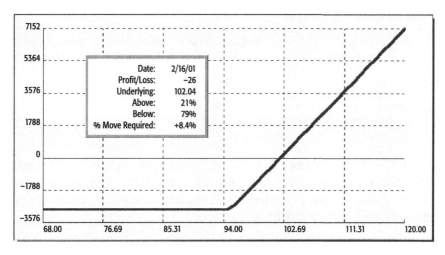

Figure 2.8 Risk curve for buying 4 February 95 calls at 7.12.

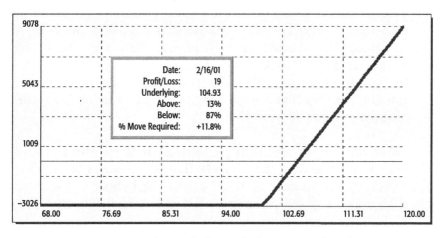

Figure 2.9 Risk curve for buying 6 February 100 calls at 4.88.

Table 2.3 displays the break-even price for each trade, the percentage move required to reach the break-even point, and the probability of that price level being reached at the time of option expiration. The obvious trend to note is that the further out-of-the-money the strike price of the option is, the lower the probability of generating a profit.

Table 2.3   Break-Even Analysis

Trade Entered	Stock Break-Even Price	Percentage Move Required	Probability of Reaching Break-Even
Buy 3 February 90 calls at 9.88	99.88	+6.2%	27%
Buy 4 February 95 calls at 7.12	102.12	+8.4%	21%
Buy 6 February 100 calls at 4.88	104.88	+11.8%	13%

Table 2.4 displays the expected dollar and percentage return for each trade based on different movements in the underlying stock. From the returns displayed in this example we can make the following observations:

- If you are highly confident that the stock is going to explode sharply higher, the February 100 call offers the greatest leverage if your opinion turns out to be correct.
- The February 90 call is the only option (in this example) that will not lose 100% if the stock is unchanged at expiration. In addition, if the stock rises 15% or even 30%, the 90 call will outperform the 95 call.
- In sum, the February 100 call offers the greatest profit potential, and the February 90 call offers the most favorable trade-off between reward and risk.

From all the information presented on these three trades, there is no way to state definitively that one trade is better than the other. Just as beauty is in the eye of the beholder, the criteria that make a given trade more attractive than another vary

Table 2.4   Expected Returns

Trade Entered	Stock Down −30%	Stock Down −15%	Stock Unchanged	Stock Up +15%	Stock Up +30%
Buy 3 February 90 calls at 9.88	−$2962 (−100%)	−$2962 (−100%)	−$1762 (−59%)	+$2467 (+83%)	+$6698 (+126%)
Buy 4 February 95 calls at 7.12	−$2850 (−100%)	−$2850 (−100%)	−$2850 (−100%)	+$2390 (+84%)	+$6023 (+111%)
Buy 6 February 100 calls at 4.88	−$2925 (−100%)	−$2925 (−100%)	−$2925 (−100%)	+$1935 (+66%)	+$10395 (+255%)

from trader to trader. Nevertheless, regardless of which trade you might choose, the key to success remains the same. The trader who will succeed in the long run is the one who takes the time to analyze the various risk-versus-reward characteristics of several potential trades and then chooses the trade that best matches his or her particular objective for that trade.

Summary

In any field of endeavor, a thorough understanding of the basics is a prerequisite to success. If you are new to option trading, you should take the time to review the material in this chapter thoroughly. Once you have a firm handle on the basics, the material in the following chapters will flow much more easily and the relevance of each concept will be much more obvious as you proceed.

Chapter 3

REASONS TO TRADE OPTIONS

Because they trade based on the price action of some underlying security, be it a stock, a stock index, or a futures contract, options are referred to as *derivatives*. In other words, their characteristics derive from the price action of the underlying security. As a result, although the action of the options for a given underlying security are related to the underlying, options offer many unique opportunities that cannot be attained solely through trading the underlying security.

Before getting into the nitty-gritty of option trading, let's examine the bigger picture. The first question on the table is not "How should I trade options?" but rather "Why bother with options in the first place?" In other words, what qualities of options are so valuable that a trader should consider using options rather than simply sticking to stocks, bonds, futures, and mutual funds?

Options offer a number of extremely useful advantages over other forms of investment. At the same time, it should not be assumed that you should therefore ignore traditional investments and commit all your capital to option trading—quite the opposite. Options are best used to augment your other investments.

The Three Primary Uses of Options

There are three primary uses of options. Each of these uses offer unique benefits—and risks—that traders and investors cannot obtain from traditional investment vehicles. The three primary uses of options follow.

1. *Leveraging an opinion on market direction.* Buying an option gives a trader the ability to control 100 shares of stock or one futures contract, usually for far less money than it would cost to trade the underlying security outright. If a trader's timing is right when entering into an option trade, he or she can obtain a much higher percentage rate of return than by simply trading the underlying while risking fewer investment dollars. By buying a naked option a trader can potentially make the same dollar profit, and a much greater percentage return, than he or she might by committing the capital to buy or sell short the underlying security itself.

2. *Hedging an existing position (or generating income from a stock portfolio).* At times traders may wish to temporarily minimize or eliminate the downside risk associated with a position they presently hold without completely exiting the current position altogether. This process—referred to as hedging an existing position—can be accomplished in several different ways using options. One alternative is to buy one put option for every 100 shares of stock (or every futures contract) held. Another alternative many investors engage in is covered call writing, which reduces downside risk to a certain degree and can increase an investor's income. Covered call writing is discussed in more detail in Chapter 18.

3. *Taking advantage of neutral situations.* Taking advantage of neutral situations is an area that is entirely unique to option trading. If you buy a stock or a futures contract, that security must rise in price in order for you to profit. If you sell short a stock or sell short a futures contract, the price of that security must fall for you to profit. With the use of options, you can enter positions that can benefit from a security rising or falling and positions that benefit from a security remaining in a particular price range for a certain period. Some examples of these types of strategies are calendar spreads (see Chapter 14), straddles (see Chapter 15), vertical spreads (see Chapter 16), and butterfly spreads (see Chapter 19).

Leveraging an Opinion on Market Direction

The most common use of options is to leverage the amount of profit possible from an anticipated move by a given stock, stock index, or futures contract. Buying a call or a put option can allow a trader to

- Put up less money than would be needed to buy or sell short 100 shares of stock or to go long or short a futures contract
- Earn a much greater percentage return on a trade than would result from buying or selling short 100 shares of stock or going long or short a futures contract

To buy an option, a trader pays a premium to the option writer. The amount paid to buy the option represents the option buyer's total risk on the trade. Conversely, upside potential is unlimited. The mantra of "limited risk, unlimited profit potential" is an oft-quoted and technically accurate description. Nevertheless, as discussed in Chapter 1, there are tradeoffs associated with every potential option trade.

For the sake of example, let's consider a trader who expects the price of IBM stock to rise. With the stock trading at 94, the trader can simply buy the stock or buy a call option. Because he wants a position that is roughly equivalent to 100 shares of stock, he may consider the following possible trades:

- Buy 100 shares of IBM at 94 a share for $9400.
- Buy 2 IBM 95 call options at 7.12 for $1425.

Table 3.1 depicts the expected dollar and percentage returns that would be achieved depending on the movement of the underlying security.

Figures 3.1 and 3.2 depict graphically the expected profit or loss for both of these positions. Consider the tradeoffs involved in choosing between the trades shown in Figure 3.1. In this example, extreme moves in either direction favor the option trader. If the stock goes up 20%, the option trader will actually experience a larger dollar gain than the stock trader despite putting up only 15% as much capital as the stock trader. Also, if the stock

Table 3.1   Expected Returns at Different Price Levels

Change in Stock Price	Buy 100 Shares Cost: $9400	Buy Two 95 Call Options Cost: $1425
Stock up 20%	+$1880 (+20%)	+$2135 (+149%)
Stock up 10%	+$940 (+10%)	+$128 (+9%)
Stock unchanged	0%	–$1425 (–100%)
Stock down 10%	–$940 (–10%)	–$1425 (–100%)
Stock down 20%	–$1880 (–20%)	–$1425 (–100%)

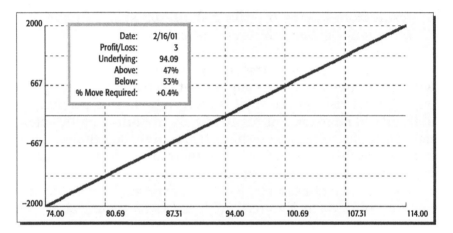

Figure 3.1   Risk curve for buying 100 shares of IBM stock at 94.

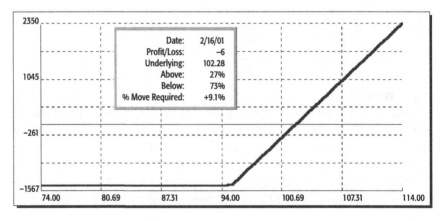

Figure 3.2   Risk curve for buying 2 IBM February 95 call options at 7.12.

drops 20%, the stock trader would be $1880 in the hole. Conversely, the option trader can lose no more than the $1425 he invested in the trade. This is true even if the stock dropped 30%, 40%, 50%, or more. Clearly, a trader who wants to maximize profitability and who is extremely confident that the stock is going to advance would want to choose the option trade.

On the other hand, if the stock stays within a narrow range through option expiration, the stock trader will come out ahead. The most dramatic example occurs if the stock is unchanged and closes at 94 on the day of option expiration. In this event, the stock trader would have no gain or loss, but the option trader would lose the entire $1425 investment on the trade.

This example clearly illustrates the tradeoffs involved in deciding whether to buy stock or a call option.

Hedging an Existing Position (and Generating Income)

Another unique and very popular use of options is to hedge an existing position. At times investors may be concerned about short-term downside risk but for various reasons (for example, tax implications) do not want to sell their positions in the underlying security. By using an option strategy, investors can reduce or even completely eliminate any downside risk beyond a certain point. To do so, investors must invariably give up some upside profit potential, at least in the short term.

Possibly the most commonly used option trading strategy, after simply buying naked calls and puts, is known as covered call writing. This strategy is detailed in Chapter 18, but we will discuss it here briefly. A trader writes a covered call by selling short, that is, writing a call option on a stock (or futures contract) that she already holds. By writing this option, the trader

- Receives the option premium, which is hers to keep whether the stock goes up or down
- In effect agrees to sell 100 shares of stock (or one futures contract) at the option's strike price, even if the stock rises above the strike price
- Retains the right to buy back the option (possibly at a loss) if she does not want the stock to get called away

Consider the following example. Trader A holds 100 shares of IBM stock, which is presently trading at 94. Trader B also holds 100 shares of stock and decides to write a covered call. He writes one February 100 call option and receives a price of 4.50, or $450. If IBM is trading at 100 or below as of option expiration, the trader will keep the entire $450 premium received. To better appreciate the allure of writing covered calls, consider this: If a trader could execute this trade four times per year, he could potentially generate up to $1800 worth of income. This represents a 19.1% return even if the stock price remains unchanged.

Trader A holds 100 shares of IBM at 94 for $9400.
Trader B holds 100 shares of IBM at 94, sells 1 IBM 100 call option at 4.50.

Table 3.2 depicts the expected dollar and percentage returns that would be achieved depending on the movement of the underlying security.

Notice the tradeoffs involved in choosing between these trades. In this example, a sharp rise in the price of IBM stock favors Trader A because Trader B, by virtue of selling a call with a strike price of 100—thereby agreeing to sell his stock at that price—gives up any profit potential above a price of 100. Nevertheless, if the stock were called away, Trader B would still earn an 11% return in 42 days or less, which represents an attractive annualized rate of return. If the stock stays in a narrow range, Trader B comes out ahead by virtue of having taken in the option premium of $450. If the stock falls, Trader B will always come out at least slightly ahead of Trader A, once again by virtue of

Table 3.2 Expected Returns at Different Price Levels

Change in Stock Price	Buy 100 Shares	Buy 100 Shares, Short 1 Call
Stock up 20%	+$1880 (+20%)	+$1050 (+11%)
Stock up 10%	+$940 (+10%)	+$1050 (+11%)
Stock unchanged	0%	+$450 (+6%)
Stock down 10%	−$940 (−10%)	−$490 (−5%)
Stock down 20%	−$1880 (−20%)	−$1430 (−15%)

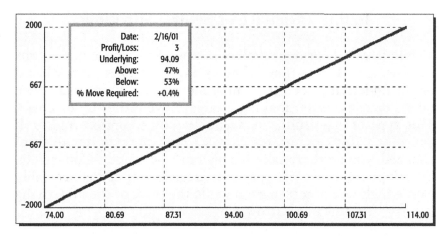

Figure 3.3   Risk curve for buying 100 shares of IBM stock at 94.

having received the option premium of $450. Nevertheless, if the stock falls too far, both traders will face the prospect of a large loss and may need to act in order to cut the loss. The bottom line is that as a hedging strategy, covered call writing offers only limited downside protection (see Figures 3.3 and 3.4).

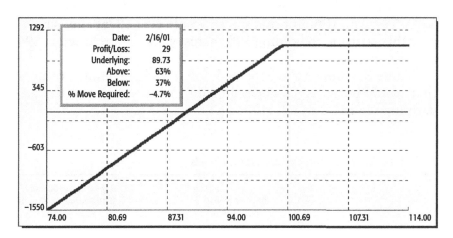

Figure 3.4   Risk curve for buying 100 shares of IBM stock at 94 and writing 1 February 100 call option at 4.50.

Taking Advantage of Neutral Situations

A unique use of options involves taking advantage of neutral situations, that is, situations whereby a trader makes money based on an underlying security remaining within a particular price range, or conversely, making a large move either up or down. This type of opportunity is available only to option traders. If you buy a stock or futures contract and its price remains unchanged, you neither make money nor lose money. Conversely, by using one of several option strategies, you can conceivably earn a high rate of return even while the price of the underlying security remains in a narrow range.

One example of a neutral strategy is known as a *calendar spread*. To establish a calendar spread an option trader buys a call (or put) option in a further-off expiration month and simultaneously writes an option with the same strike price for a nearer-term month. This strategy is covered in detail in Chapter 14, but the basic idea is that the near-term option loses value more quickly than the longer-term option, thus generating a profit.

As an example of a calendar spread, you could buy the April 95 IBM call option at a price of 10.50 and simultaneously write the February 95 IBM call option at a price of 6.75. To enter this trade you would pay the difference in price of 3.75 points, or $375. To buy a 10-lot of this spread would cost $3750. Let's compare this position to holding 100 shares of stock purchased at $94 a share.

Table 3.3 shows the expected dollar and percentage returns that would be achieved depending on the movement of the underlying security.

Table 3.3   Expected Returns at Different Price Levels

Change in Stock Price	Buy 100 Shares Cost: $9400	Buy 10 April 100 Calls Sell 10 February 100 Calls Cost: $3750
Stock up 20%	+$1880 (+20%)	−$560 (−15%)
Stock up 10%	+$940 (+10%)	+$1590 (+42%)
Stock unchanged	0%	+$4080 (+109%)
Stock down 10%	−$940 (−10%)	−$70 (−2%)
Stock down 20%	−$1880 (−20%)	−$2430 (−65%)

Notice the stark contrast in returns for these two positions at each price level. Whereas the long stock position makes money if the stock rises and loses money if the stock falls, the option position

- Makes money if the stock remains relatively unchanged
- Incurs losses if the stock makes a significant move in either direction (see Figures 3.5 and 3.6)

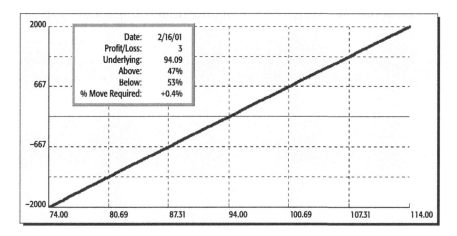

Figure 3.5   Risk curve for buying 100 shares of IBM stock at 94.

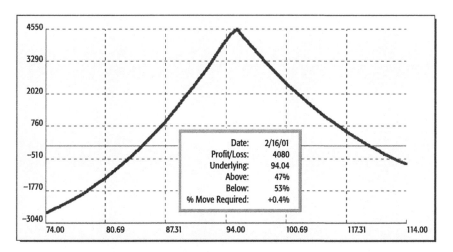

Figure 3.6   Risk curve for buying 10 April 100 calls and writing 10 February 100 Calls.

Summary

Each of the trades discussed in this chapter offer unique opportunities to astute traders. Each strategy also entails unique risks, which must be understood and accounted for if you hope to use them successfully. More information on how to use these strategies is provided in Chapters 12 through 19. For now, the main point to understand is that the potential rewards and risks associated with these strategies are unique to option trading and cannot be duplicated solely by trading the underlying security itself.

Chapter 4

OPTION PRICING

The price for a given option in the marketplace is determined primarily by supply and demand. In other words, unless a buyer and a seller of a particular option are willing to consummate a trade at an agreed-on price, there is no trade. As discussed in Chapter 9, when you actually go to enter a trade you are quoted a bid price and an ask price. If you want to buy an option at the current market price, you pay the *ask* price. If you want to sell an option at the current market price, you receive the *bid* price. These bid and ask prices are generally quoted by traders known as *market makers*, who make their living by buying and selling options for a given security or group of securities.

For stock options the spread between the bid and ask price can range anywhere from one-eighth of a point to a full point or more. This spread can have a profound effect on your actual trading results. The size of this spread varies based on such factors as volume, volatility, and the raw price of the option itself. If an option on a $25 stock is 20 points out of the money, the price of the option will be very low and so will the bid-ask spread. Generally, the more actively traded an option, the tighter the bid-ask spread. Conversely, an option that is 20 points in the money may be bid at a price of 21 and offered at a price of 22.

Theoretical Value

In most cases the market price for an option is slightly above to slightly below the *theoretical* price for that option, which is also referred to as *fair value*. In the early days of option trading, there was no such thing as fair value. The market makers for the options on a particular security would set a price and other traders could either pay this price or simply not trade. Eventually several scholars got together and developed a formula for determining a fair price for a given option, based on a set of current variables.

The most commonly used model is the Black-Scholes model, named after its developers. Another commonly used option model is the binomial model, which uses a complex series of iterative calculations to arrive at its version of fair value for a given option. There are several other variations, but by and large the theoretical prices calculated by various option models are generally very close in value. In each case, the inputs used to determine an option's theoretical price are roughly the same:

A. The current price of the underlying security
B. The strike price of the option under analysis
C. Current interest rates
D. The number of days until the option expires
E. A volatility value

Elements A through E are passed to an option pricing model, which then generates a *theoretical option price*. (Note that stock dividends also play a role in option models, but this element is omitted here for simplicity.)

Elements A, B, C, and D are known variables. In other words, at any given point in time one can readily observe the underlying price, the strike price for the option in question, the current level of interest rates, and the number of days until the option expires. In selecting a volatility value to use in the option model calculation, the most commonly used choice is the actual historic volatility of the underlying security. Historical volatility is discussed in more detail in Chapter 6, but in general terms, historic volatility measures the standard deviation of underlying price changes during a given period in order to calculate an estimate of how much that security is likely to rise or fall within the next 12 months. For example, a stock with a historical volatility of 30 would be expected to rise or fall within a range of plus or minus 30% in the next 12 months. Similarly, a stock with a historical volatility of 80 would be expected to rise or fall within a range of plus or minus 80% in the next 12 months.

As will become more clear between here and the end of Chapter 8, the level of volatility inherent in the underlying security has a profound effect on the prices for options on that security.

Examples of Theoretical Option Pricing

The following example illustrates the factors that go into calculating a theoretical option price. Let's assume the following variables for a particular underlying stock:

Current date	February 12, 2001
Current price of the underlying security	99
Strike price of the option under analysis	100
Current interest rate	5
Number of days until the option expires	33
Volatility	30

Given these inputs, the Black-Scholes option model would return the following theoretical call and put prices for the March 2001 100 call and put options:

Theoretical 100 call price	3.32
Theoretical 100 put price	3.92

Table 4.1 uses the same variables as the previous example, except for the volatility value. Table 4.1 shows the theoretical price for both the 100 call and put options for five different volatility levels. Volatility is increased from 10 to 50 in increments of 10, with all other variables held constant. Note the profound effect these changes in volatility have on the theoretical option prices calculated by the option model.

Table 4.1   The Effect of Volatility on Theoretical Option Prices

Underlying Price	Strike Price	Interest Rate	Days to Expiration	Volatility	Theoretical Call Price	Theoretical Put Price
99	100	5	33	10	0.93	1.55
99	100	5	33	20	2.14	2.73
99	100	5	33	30	3.32	3.92
99	100	5	33	40	4.51	5.10
99	100	5	33	50	5.69	6.28

Table 4.2 displays the theoretical and actual market prices and the difference between the two for IBM options on January 5. Note that the options with strike prices closest to the current stock price—the 90, 95, and 100 strike price options—show the smallest difference between theoretical and actual prices. This is a common phenomenon because the near-the-money options tend to have the greatest volume and so tend to be the most accurately priced options for each security.

Overvalued Options versus Undervalued Options

If the actual market price for an option is above the theoretical price for that option, that option is considered overvalued. In theory, a trader can gain a slight edge by writing options that are overvalued. Conversely, if the actual market price of an option is below the theoretical price for that option, that option is considered undervalued. In theory, a trader gains a slight edge by buying options that are undervalued and/or writing options that are overvalued. Traders should be forewarned, however, not to expect to make a living buying undervalued options and writing overvalued options. Many other factors are involved that can quickly wipe out any theoretical edge. For example, if a trader buys an undervalued call and the underlying stock subsequently plummets, that option is going to decline in price anyway.

In Table 4.2, overvalued options are noted by a negative Diff. value (differential) and undervalued options are noted by a positive Diff. value.

Table 4.2   IBM Options on January 5 with IBM Trading at 94 (Theoretical Price versus Actual Price)

		Calls						Puts			
		JAN 14	FEB 42	APR 106	JUL 197			JAN 14	FEB 42	APR 106	JUL 197
80	Theoretical	14.70	16.23	18.77	21.39	80	Theoretical	.54	1.78	3.62	5.26
	Market	15.25	16.50	19.75	21.50		Market	1.38	2.38	4.25	5.62
	Difference	-.55	-.27	-.98	-.11		Difference	-.84	-.60	-.63	-.36
85	Theoretical	10.56	12.61	19.75	21.50	85	Theoretical	1.39	3.13	5.32	7.14
	Market	11.12	13.00	15.75	18.50		Market	2.06	3.62	5.88	7.38
	Difference	-.56	-.39	-.21	-.10		Difference	-.67	-.49	-.56	-.24
90	Theoretical	7.10	9.53	12.72	15.73	90	Theoretical	2.93	5.02	7.42	9.34
	Market	7.88	9.50	13.12	15.75		Market	3.50	5.12	7.88	9.88
	Difference	-.78	-.03	-.40	-.02		Difference	-.57	-.10	-.46	-.54
95	Theoretical	4.46	7.02	10.31	13.39	95	Theoretical	5.28	7.47	9.94	11.86
	Market	4.50	6.88	10.12	13.25		Market	5.25	7.62	10.12	12.00
	Difference	-.04	-.14	.19	.14		Difference	.03	-.15	-.18	-.14
100	Theoretical	2.61	5.03	8.26	11.34	100	Theoretical	8.42	10.45	12.82	14.67
	Market	2.38	4.75	8.00	10.88		Market	8.12	10.12	12.50	14.38
	Difference	.23	.28	.26	.46		Difference	.30	.33	.32	.29
105	Theoretical	1.42	3.52	6.56	9.56	105	Theoretical	12.22	13.92	16.05	17.76
	Market	1.31	3.00	6.12	8.88		Market	12.50	13.38	16.25	17.38
	Difference	.11	.52	.44	.68		Difference	-.28	.54	-.20	.38
110	Theoretical	.73	2.41	5.17	8.03	110	Theoretical	16.52	17.78	19.59	21.10
	Market	.62	2.00	4.88	7.50		Market	17.00	17.75	19.12	20.62
	Difference	.11	.41	.29	.53		Difference	-.48	.03	.47	.48

Table 4.3 Theoretical Prices for 95 Call (Current Option Price = 6.5, Current Underlying Price = 94)

	Days until Expiration							
	37	32	27	22	17	12	7	2
112.81	20.00	19.63	19.25	18.94	18.56	18.25	18.00	17.88
108.12	16.13	15.69	15.25	14.81	14.38	13.88	13.44	13.19
103.43	12.56	12.13	11.63	11.06	10.50	9.88	9.19	8.56
98.68	9.38	8.88	8.31	7.75	7.13	6.38	5.50	4.38
94.00	6.69	6.19	5.63	5.06	4.38	3.69	2.75	1.50
89.31	4.50	4.00	3.50	3.00	2.44	1.81	1.06	0.25
84.62	2.81	2.38	2.00	1.56	1.19	0.75	0.31	0.00
79.93	1.56	1.31	1.00	0.75	0.44	0.25	0.06	0.0

Table 4.3 displays the expected theoretical price for the IBM February 95 call option over one period and through a range of underlying prices. For this display, volatility and interest rates are held constant. The range of stock prices is listed down the left side of the grid and the number of days left until expiration across the top of the grid. Note that as the underlying price increases, so does the option price. Conversely, as the price of the stock falls, so does the price of the option. Notice how the option price decreases (or decays) with the passage of time, even if the underlying price is held constant. This is an illustration of time decay, which is discussed in greater detail in Chapter 5.

Summary: Theory versus Reality

It is important to understand how options are priced and to be able to recognize if a particular option is overvalued (i.e., trading above its theoretical value) or undervalued (i.e., trading below its theoretical value). Nevertheless, in the real world of trading this information often becomes somewhat moot. For instance, suppose you are bullish on a given stock and have selected a call option that you want to buy. Just before you place an order to buy the option you realize that the ask price for the option is 5.00, but according to your option pricing model the theoretical price or fair value for the option is only 4.25. Now you are faced with a choice. Do you pay a price that is theoretically too high for the option, or do you skip the trade altogether? If you buy the option anyway and the underlying security fails to make a big move, you will suffer an even bigger loss than you would if you had been able to buy the option at fair value. If you skip the trade altogether and the underlying security makes the huge move you expected, you will have missed out on a large profit for fear of risking a few dollars more.

In sum, it is important to be aware of the price of a given option in the marketplace relative to the fair value calculated for that option by an option pricing model. However, in the real world the currently available bid and ask prices have a much greater impact on your success or failure than the theoretical value for a given option.

Chapter 5

TIME DECAY

If an option is trading in the money before expiration, the price of that option comprises intrinsic value plus time premium. If an option is trading out of the money before expiration, the price of that option is made up solely of time premium.

The amount of time premium built into the price of any given option depends on the option pricing variables discussed in Chapter 4. In other words, the amount of time left until expiration, the volatility, the amount by which the option is in or out of the money, and the current level of interest rates are all factors influencing the amount of time premium built into the price of each option.

The time premium built into any option decays at an ever faster rate as option expiration draws nearer. Most commonly referred to as time decay, this phenomenon can have a profound effect on many option trades that a trader might consider.

As a trader it is important to understand and accept the fact that once an option reaches expiration, there will be no time premium left in its price. If the option is trading in the money at the time of expiration, the price of that option will be equal to the difference between the price of the underlying stock or futures market and the strike price of the option. If the option is trading out of the money at the time of expiration, it will be worthless.

Because of this mathematical fact we can state that there are three great certainties in life:

- Death.
- Taxes.
- Every option will lose all of its time premium at expiration.

Understanding the effect that time decay can have on each trade you make is one of the keys to consistently putting the odds on your side trade after trade. Traders who are not concerned about time decay are almost certain to fail in the long run because too often they will be betting on a long shot—often without even knowing they are doing so. Although this may sound foreboding to some, the underlying concept is extremely simple:

- If you buy premium, time premium decay works *against* you.
- If you sell premium, time premium decay works *for* you.

This is not to imply that you should always write options or that you should never buy options. What it means is that if you hope to succeed in option trading, you must understand these two tenets and take steps to maximize the potential benefits and minimize the potential negative effect that time decay can have on your option positions.

The best way to illustrate the effect and importance of time decay is with an example. Let us assume the following hypothetical situation. On August 18, the stock of IBM is trading at a price of 120. A trader wishes to buy the October 120 call, which has 63 days left until expiration. The price of the option purchased is 8.44. For the sake of argument—and to highlight time decay as the only key variable in this example—we assume that at the end of each subsequent week IBM is still trading at a price of 120 and that volatility is unchanged.

The Effect of Time Decay on the Price of an Option

Table 5.1 and Figures 5.2 and 5.3 each show the effect of time decay on the price of the IBM October 120 call in a slightly different format. Table 5.1 displays numerically the expected price of the option at the end of each week as well as the percentage

Table 5.1   Option Price and Percentage Change Week by Week

Date	Option Price	% Lost to Time Decay
8/18	8.44	—
8/25	7.94	–5.9%
9/1	7.38	–7.1%
9/8	6.82	–7.6%
9/15	6.19	–9.2%
9/22	5.50	–11.1%
9/29	4.75	–13.6%
10/6	3.88	–18.4%
10/13	2.75	–29.0%
10/20	0.00	–100.0%

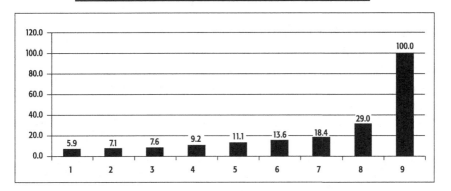

Figure 5.1   Percentage of option price lost to time decay week by week.

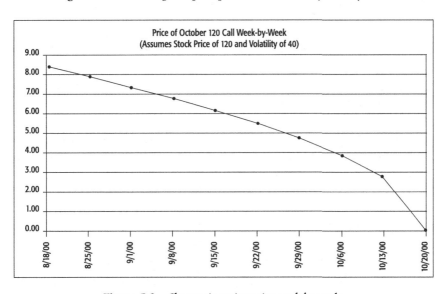

Figure 5.2   Changes in option price week by week.

loss from the previous week's closing price. Figure 5.1 shows the percentage loss from the previous week's closing price in graphical form. Figure 5.2 shows the price of the option at the end of each week. The key elements to note are these:

- Time decay is an inevitable and progressive process.
- The rate at which the time premium in an option price decays accelerates as expiration draws nearer.

Implications of Time Decay

There are several implications of time decay that a trader must recognize and account for when planning and executing trades. Most notably, if you buy an option, you must expect to lose a portion of the price of your option as time goes by. You must hope that the underlying security moves far enough in the direction that you expect it to in order to compensate for this loss of time premium. If you are an option writer, you can expect time decay to work in your favor as time goes by. As an option writer, your primary concern is that the underlying price will move against you and create losses in excess of the amount you gain from time decay.

Time Decay Illustrated

Although a textbook understanding of time decay and its effect on the price of an option may be interesting and important, for a trader it is most important to understand the effect it will have on a given trade. The net effect of time decay to you as an option buyer is that with each passing day and week, the break-even price for your trade moves further away.

Figures 5.3 through 5.7 illustrate the negative effect of time decay for the option buyer. Notice how each successive risk curve moves slightly lower and farther to the right (i.e., the break-even price moves a little further away each week) as some of the time premium paid by the option buyer evaporates. This

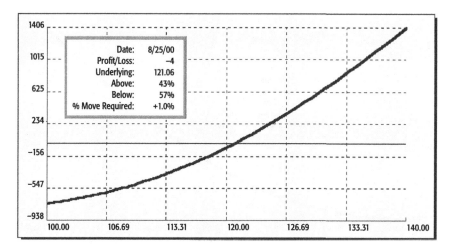

Figure 5.3 IBM October 120 call as of 8/25/00.

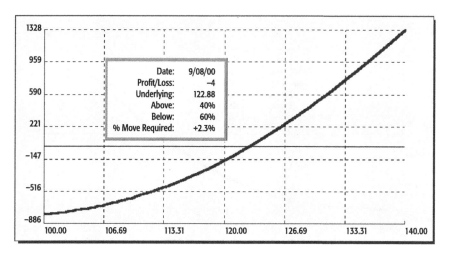

Figure 5.4 IBM October 120 call as of 9/8/00.

means that for each week that passes, the probability of reaching the break-even price declines slightly.

A key point to note (see Figure 5.8) is that if you buy an option, you will make more money if the underlying security's price rises sooner rather than later. In this example, if IBM shot

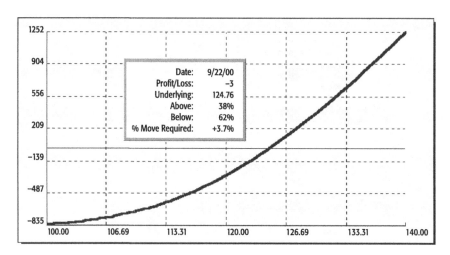

Figure 5.5 IBM October 120 call as of 9/22/00.

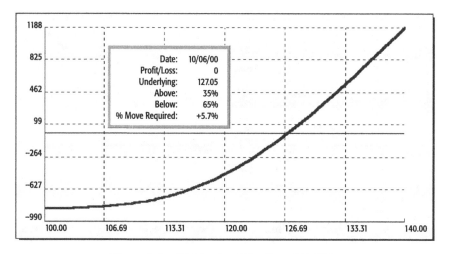

Figure 5.6 IBM October 120 call as of 10/6/00.

up from 120 to 140 in one week, the buyer of this option would expect to have a profit of $1406. Conversely, if the stock rises to 140 by expiration on October 20, the profit would be only $1156.

Table 5.2 illustrates numerically the negative effect of time decay. Assuming that as of each date, the price of IBM stock is

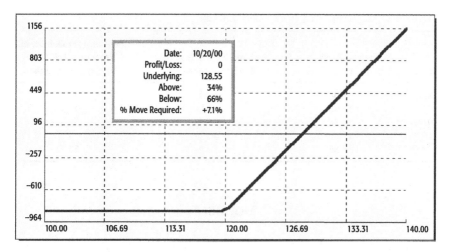

Figure 5.7　IBM October 120 call as of 10/20/00.

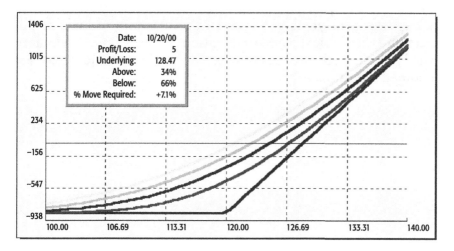

Figure 5.8　IBM October 120 call (the effect of time decay).

120, notice how time decay in the price of the option causes the break-even price to move farther away. Thus, with each passing week, the percentage move required for the stock to reach the break-even price increases and the probability of reaching the price declines.

Table 5.2   Expectations for IBM October 120 Call

Date	Underlying Break-Even Price	Percentage Move Required to Reach Break-Even Price	Percentage Probability of Reaching Break-Even Price by Indicated Date
8/22	121.06	1.0%	43%
9/8	122.88	2.3%	40%
9/22	124.76	3.7%	38%
10/6	127.05	5.7%	35%
10/20	128.55	7.1%	34%

Summary

Time decay is a factor involved in virtually every single option trade. Depending on the strategy you use and the specific options that you buy or sell, time decay may have a vastly favorable or unfavorable impact on your trade. If you do not yet understand why this is true, you should review this chapter until you do understand this critical element of option trading. Traders who routinely trade with no concern for the effect of time decay are doomed to failure.

Chapter 6

VOLATILITY

Volatility: The Most Important Concept in Option Trading

Understanding the concept of volatility is essential to option trading success. A trader who can recognize whether a given option or series of options is cheap or expensive on a historic basis has a tremendous advantage in the marketplace. Flexible traders can buy premium when volatilities are low and sell premium when volatilities are high. They can establish spreads in which they buy inexpensive options and sell expensive options, thus obtaining the best of both worlds. These are key steps in consistently placing the odds as far in your favor as possible.

To gain a meaningful understanding of volatility as it relates to option trading, we must address three topics:

1. Historical (or statistical) volatility
2. Implied option volatility
3. Relative volatility

Historical Volatility Explained

Historical volatility, also referred to as *calculated* or *statistical* volatility, is simply a measure of the price fluctuations of the underlying security (a stock, an index, or a futures contract) over a specific period. For example, one can calculate the standard deviation of the S&P 500 over the last 20 days to determine the 20-day historical volatility. Some traders then plug this historical volatility value into an option model to calculate theoretical prices for the options on that security. If historical volatility is 30%, the implication is that the underlying security is likely to rise or fall within a range of plus or minus 30% from the current price within the following 12 months.

Figure 6.1A displays the 20-day historical volatility for IBM from 1994 through 2000. Note that because the method is always looking at the last 20 days of data, the values can swing widely from high to low.

To get a more useful picture it can be helpful to look at the same data with a moving average and one or more standard deviation bands drawn above and below the moving average. A moving average helps to smooth out the short-term fluctuations and makes it easier to identify extremely high- or low-volatility situations.

Figure 6.1B shows the same graph as in Figure 6.1A with a 500-day moving average drawn through the data. Also shown are a band that is 1.5 standard deviations above the moving average and a band 1.5 standard deviations below the moving average.

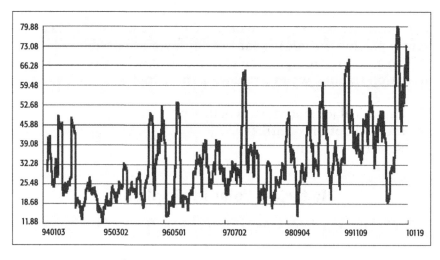

Figure 6.1A   IBM 20-day historical (or statistical) volatility.

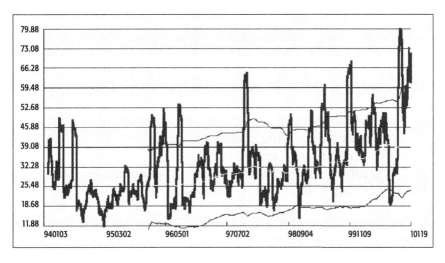

Figure 6.1B   IBM 20-day historical (or statistical) volatility with average.

Implied Volatility Explained

Although historical volatility can be of some value, the more important type of volatility for option trading is *implied volatility*. The primary difference between historical and implied volatility is that historical volatility is based on the past price movements of the underlying security, whereas implied volatility is based on the current market prices for the options for that underlying security. Historical volatility looks backward at what has already happened, but implied volatility reflects the marketplace's current expectations for future volatility.

The implied volatility value for a given option is the value that one would need to plug into an option pricing model in order to generate the current market price of an option, given that the other variables are already known. (The known variables are underlying price, days to expiration, interest rates, and the difference between the option's strike price and the price of the underlying security.) In other words, implied volatility is the volatility implied by the current market price for a given option.

Calculating Implied Volatility for a Given Option

As discussed in Chapter 4, several variables are entered into an option pricing model in order to arrive at a theoretical price, or fair value, for a given option:

A. The current price of the underlying security
B. The strike price of the option under analysis
C. A current interest rate
D. The number of days until the option expires
E. A volatility value

Elements A through E are passed to an option pricing model, which then generates

F. A theoretical option price

Elements A, B, C, and D are known variables. In other words, at any given point in time one can readily observe the underlying price, the strike price for the option in question, the current level of interest rates, and the number of days left until the option expires. To calculate the implied volatility of a given option, we follow the procedure detailed above, with one significant modification. Instead of passing elements A through E to an option pricing model to have the model generate a theoretical price, we pass elements A through D along with the actual market price for the option as variable F, and then allow the option pricing model to solve for element E, the volatility value. A computer is needed to make this calculation.

This volatility value is called the implied volatility for that option. In other words, it is the volatility that is implied by the marketplace based on the actual price of the option. For example, on 1/5/2001 the IBM February 2001 95 call option was trading at a price of 6.88. The variables are as follows:

A. The current price of the underlying security = 94
B. The strike price of the option under analysis = 95
C. Current interest rates   = 5
D. The number of days until the option expires   = 42

E. Volatility = ?
F. The actual market price of the option = 6.88

The unknown variable that must be solved for is element E, volatility. Given the variables listed above, a volatility value of 56.20 must be plugged into element E for the option pricing model to generate a theoretical price that equals the actual market price of 6.88 (this value of 56.20 can be calculated only by passing the other variables into an option pricing model). Thus, as of the close on January 5, the implied volatility for the IBM February 2001 95 call is 56.20.

Measuring Implied Volatility for Options on a Given Security

Different options for the same underlying security can and usually do trade at different implied volatility levels. If demand for a given option is great, the price of that option may be driven to artificially high levels, thus resulting in a higher implied volatility for that option. The differences in implied volatilities across strike prices among options of the same expiration month for a given underlying is referred to as the volatility *skew*. The topic of volatility skew is discussed in more detail later in this chapter.

Table 6.1 displays the implied volatility values for IBM options on January 5. There are several key features to note in this example:

- For each expiration month the volatility level tends to decrease as the strike price increases. This is an example of a skew.
- The average volatility value for each successive expiration month is lower than the previous expiration month. This can lead to good opportunities for traders to buy options of the further-off expiration month and sell the near-term options.
- Each option trades at a different implied volatility level.

Although each option for a given underlying security may trade at its own implied volatility level, it is possible to calculate a single value that can be referred to as the *average implied*

Table 6.1 Implied Volatilities for IBM Options

	Calls					Puts			
	JAN 14	FEB 42	APR 106	JUL 197		JAN 14	FEB 42	APR 106	JUL 197
70	101.13	70.62	58.97	51.95	70	NA	68.50	59.02	51.47
75	95.69	65.68	57.04	51.18	75	90.02	66.45	55.68	50.77
80	87.31	62.97	55.06	48.52	80	85.73	63.15	54.00	49.13
85	80.97	60.47	52.90	47.79	85	77.69	60.38	53.06	48.33
90	74.45	58.11	51.70	47.33	90	72.37	59.25	51.63	47.41
95	67.23	56.20	50.59	45.79	95	68.00	57.52	50.27	46.36
100	64.19	54.09	49.29	45.52	100	64.29	56.15	49.90	45.65
105	62.47	53.31	48.95	44.75	105	66.27	54.25	50.00	45.81
110	64.61	51.91	48.33	44.77	110	71.45	54.00	49.13	45.91
115	60.86	50.47	47.77	44.45	115	70.08	54.29	49.45	46.65
120	NA	49.88	47.65	43.50	120	NA	54.59	50.00	47.15

volatility value for the options on that security for a specific day. This average value for the current day can then be compared to the historic range of average daily implied volatility values for that security to determine if the current value is high, low, or somewhere in between. This knowledge can then be used to help determine which trading strategy to employ.

The simplest method available is to calculate the average implied volatility of the at-the-money call and the at-the-money put for the nearest expiration month that has more than two weeks left until expiration, and to refer to that value as the implied volatility for that security. The basis for using this method is that the at-the-money options are generally the most actively traded and serve as a reliable reference point when approximating option volatility levels for a given security. For example, if IBM is trading at 94 on December 31, the implied volatility for the February 95 call is 56.20, and the implied volatility for the February 95 put is 57.52, then using this method one can objectively state that IBM's implied volatility equals 56.86 [(56.20 + 57.52)/2]. The primary advantage of this method is that it is quite simple to use. The primary disadvantage is that it assumes that the volatilities of all the options on that security are in line with the near month's at-the-money options. Though this is generally accurate, it is a fairly broad assumption. At times there can be wide variations in the volatility level of different options.

Another method for arriving at a single daily implied volatility value for the options of a given underlying security is to take the average implied volatility of all the options on that security, including all expiration months and all strike prices. The advantage of this method is that it takes into account all the securities' options. The disadvantage is that sometimes many far-out-of-the-money options or options that rarely trade are included in the mix, which can give too much weight to thinly traded options.

A third method, which is a compromise between the first two, involves including all expiration months and all options trading within two or three strikes of the at-the-money option. In the long run this method generally results in the most consistent results since it includes the options that are generally most actively traded and are thus the most accurately priced.

Ultimately, the method used to arrive at a daily implied volatility value for a given security is not all that critical as long as the same method is used every day. The purpose of calculating this daily aggregate value is to compare it to previous readings for that security to assess whether implied option volatility is currently high or low. This leads us to the concept of relative volatility.

Is Implied Volatility High or Low? Relative Volatility Explained

The purpose of relative volatility ranking is to allow traders to determine objectively whether the current level of implied option volatility for the options on a given stock or commodity is high, low, or somewhere in between on a historic basis. This knowledge can be extremely useful and is key in determining the best trading strategies to employ at any given time for a given security.

The most useful method for calculating relative volatility is to take all the previous daily readings for implied volatility for a given security over the last two years and to sort the values from highest to lowest. This sorted list is then cut into 10 equal increments, or deciles. If the current implied volatility is in the lowest decile, relative volatility rank is 1, indicating that the options on this security are cheap. If the current implied volatility is in the highest decile, relative volatility rank is 10, indicating that the options on this security are expensive. To put it another way:

- If 90% or more of the daily readings in the last two years were *greater than* the current day's reading, the current relative volatility rank would be 1.
- If 90% or more of the daily readings in the last two years were *less than* the current day's reading, the current relative volatility rank would be 10.

This technique allows traders to make an objective determination as to whether implied option volatility is currently high or low for a given security.

Figure 6.2 displays the daily implied volatility reading for IBM for two years. During this two-year period, implied volatil-

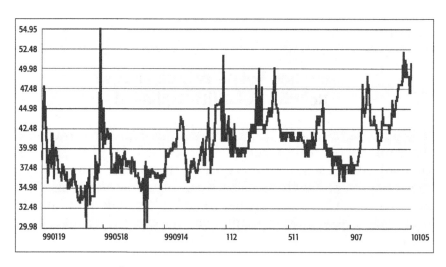

Figure 6.2   Average implied volatility for IBM options (daily).

ity ranged from a high of almost 55 to a low just under 30. The current reading of approximately 50 is clearly at the high end of all readings during the period. As a result, on January 5, IBM options would be assigned a relative volatility rank of 10. As we will soon discuss, the knowledge that option premium is high should have an effect on traders' decisions about which trading strategies to consider, as well as the specific trades they enter.

Note that as of the last date on the graphs in Figures 6.2 and 6.3, the raw levels of implied option volatility for IBM and Merrill Lynch are very close. IBM volatility is about 50 and Merrill Lynch volatility is about 45. Yet clearly, based on the historic range of implied volatility for each stock, volatility is high for IBM options and low for Merrill Lynch options.

Making this critical determination is the key purpose of analyzing relative volatility. Without examining the data on these graphs, the novice trader might incorrectly assume that the same trading strategies should be applied to both stocks. Yet because implied volatility is high for IBM options, a trader would generally be better off considering option-writing strategies. Conversely, because implied volatility is low for Merrill Lynch

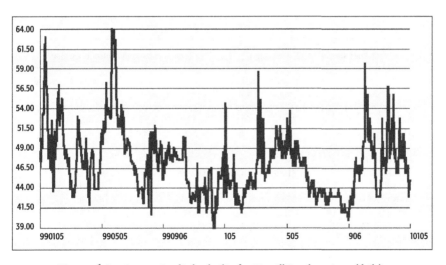

Figure 6.3   Average implied volatility for Merrill Lynch options (daily).

options, a trader would generally be better off considering option-buying strategies.

Relative Volatility Ranking

Figure 6.4 displays the implied volatility level (Implied Vol.) and relative volatility rank (Relative Vol.) for a list of stocks and futures markets. As discussed in the strategy chapters, it is often useful to consider one set of strategies for securities that trade at a low volatility rank and another set of strategies for securities trading at a high volatility rank.

Considerations in Selecting Option-Trading Strategies

Current Implied Volatility and Relative Volatility Rank

If relative volatility is low for a given security (on a scale of 1 to 10), traders can benefit from focusing on buy premium strategies and are generally advised to avoid writing options. Conversely,

Stock Option Volatility Ranking			Commodity Option Volatility Ranking		
Name	Implied Vol.	Relative Vol.	Name	Implied Vol.	Relative Vol.
ALCOA	24.31	4	BRITISH_POUND	8.24	4
ALTERA_INC	45.87	3	CANADIAN_DOLLAR	3.36	1
AMD	53.85	4	CATTLE_FEEDER	13.66	4
AMER_EXPR	24.92	4	CATTLE_LIVE	13.27	3
AMER_ONLINE	71.30	4	COCOA	13.56	1
AMGEN	34.34	4	COFFEE	31.49	5
ANN_TAYLOR	55.58	3	COPPER	30.35	5
APPLE_COMPUTER	41.77	3	CORN	17.93	3
APPLIED_MATERIALS	45.44	2	COTTON	17.63	4
ASA	21.59	3	CRB_INDEX	8.43	5

Figure 6.4 Average implied volatilities and relative volatility rankings.

when relative volatility is high, traders should focus on sell premium strategies and are generally advised to avoid buying options.

This simple filtering method is a critical first step in making money in options in the long run. The best way to find the good trades is to filter out the bad trades. Buying premium when volatility is high and selling premium when volatility is low are low-probability trades, as they put the odds immediately against you. Avoiding these low-probability trades allows you to focus on trades that have a much greater probability of making money. Proper trade selection is one of the most important factors in trading options profitably in the long run.

Skew of Implied Volatilities

Determining the exact strategy to employ can be fine-tuned by examining the differences in the implied volatilities of various options for a given security. Often the out-of-the-money options on a given security are trading at a much higher or lower implied volatility level than the at-the-money options. These situations can create unique opportunities for astute traders by allowing them to buy low-volatility (i.e., cheap) options and write higher-volatility (i.e., expensive) options.

The pattern of differences between implied volatilities of various options is referred to as the *skew*. An upward-sloping skew indicates that out-of-the-money call options are more expensive, that is, they trade at a higher volatility. A downward-sloping skew indicates that out-of-the-money call options are cheaper than at-the-money options, that is, they trade at a lower volatility. Either situation creates opportunities for traders to buy cheap options and sell more expensive options.

Figure 6.5 displays the skew for IBM January options on January 5. The 95 option is the at-the-money strike. The graph depicts the difference between the volatility for each strike price compared to the at-the-money 95 strike. As you can see, the lower strike prices trade at higher volatilities and the volatility level declines steadily as the strike prices move higher. As an

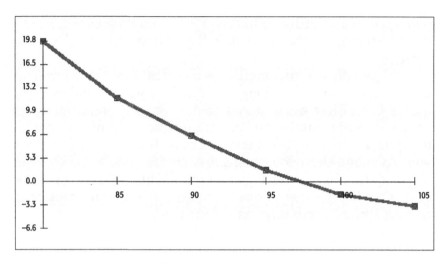

Figure 6.5   Volatility skew for IBM options.

example of how this information can be used, a trader might consider buying an at-the-money put option (the 95 strike) and simultaneously writing an out-of-the-money put option (the 85 strike, for example), which is trading at a higher volatility.

Why Does Volatility Matter?

Rather than just stating that high volatility has negative implications for option buyers, let's look at an example.

As you saw in Table 6.1, implied volatility for IBM options has ranged from 30 to 55. What implications does this information have for a trader considering buying a particular call option? Consider the following scenario: On January 8, with IBM trading at a price of 94, a trader wants to purchase the April 90 call option. What would the difference be if the volatility of that option were 30 versus 55 at the time of the purchase, and what would the implications be for the likelihood of making a profit on the trade?

In Table 6.2 you can see that if volatility were at the low end of the range, we could expect the April 90 call option to trade at (approximately) 8.80 points. Conversely, in Table 6.3 you can see that if volatility were at the high end of the range, the April

Table 6.2   IBM Theoretical Option Prices for Implied Volatility of 30

	Calls			
	JAN 11	FEB 39	APR 103	JUL 194
70	24.10	24.37	25.10	26.38
75	19.11	19.42	20.43	20.07
80	14.12	14.58	16.05	18.11
85	9.17	10.07	12.14	14.57
90	4.64	6.26	8.80	11.48
95	1.56	3.44	6.12	8.88
100	.30	1.66	4.08	6.75
105	.03	.70	2.62	5.04
110	.00	.26	1.62	3.70
115	.00	.08	.96	2.68
120	.00	.02	.55	1.92

Table 6.3   IBM Theoretical Option Prices for Implied Volatility of 55

	Calls			
	JAN 11	FEB 39	APR 103	JUL 194
70	24.10	24.65	26.72	29.63
75	19.13	20.10	22.85	26.24
80	14.26	15.90	19.33	23.15
85	9.74	12.19	16.19	20.34
90	5.94	9.05	13.44	17.82
95	3.18	6.50	11.06	15.57
100	1.47	4.53	9.03	13.57
105	.59	3.06	7.32	11.80
110	.20	2.02	5.89	10.24
115	.06	1.29	4.72	8.88
120	.01	.81	3.76	7.69

90 call option would trade at (approximately) 13.44 points, or 53% higher than if volatility were at the low end of the range. The risk curves depicted in Figures 6.6 and 6.7 illustrate the implications of buying when volatility is low rather than high.

As you can see in Figure 6.6, if a trader paid 8.80 for this call option, the break-even point would be 98.80, thus requiring a 4.7% rise in the stock price by the time of option expiration.

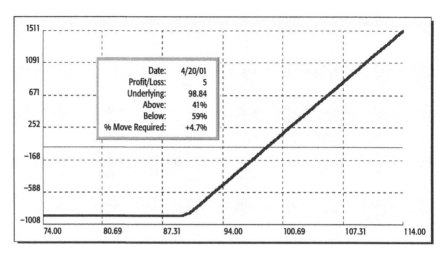

Figure 6.6 Profit/loss curve for April 90 call bought at 8.80.

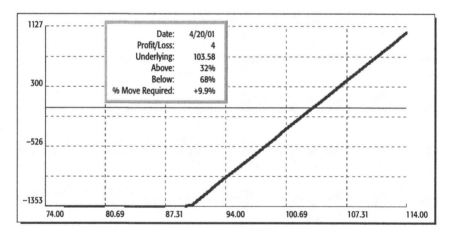

Figure 6.7 Profit/loss curve for April 90 call bought at 13.44.

Based on IBM's historic volatility at the time, there is an estimated 41% probability of this occurring.

Conversely, if the trader had paid 13.44 for the option, the break-even price would be 103.58, thus requiring a 9.9% rise in the stock by the time of option expiration. Based on IBM's historic volatility at the time, it is estimated that there is a 32% probability of this occurring (see Table 6.4).

Table 6.4 Expectations for IBM October 120 Call

Volatility and Price	Underlying Break-Even Price	% Move Required to Reach Break-Even price	% Probability of Reaching Break-Even Price by Indicated Date
30%/8.80	98.84	4.7%	41%
55%/13.44	103.58	9.9%	32%

This example clearly illustrates the importance of volatility analysis in option trading. Assessing whether the current level of implied option volatility for a given security is high or low lets you objectively measure whether the options are cheap or expensive, and by extension, to determine if option buying or option writing offers the best opportunity.

The Effect of Changes in Volatility

There is one other important aspect of volatility that traders should be aware of: Changes in volatility have a greater effect on the prices of longer-term options than on the prices of shorter-term options. In other words, if volatility rises, an option at a given strike price with five months left until expiration will increase in price much more than an option at the same strike price with only two months until expiration. If volatility declines, an option at a given strike price with five months left to expiration will decrease in price much more than an option at the same strike price with only two months left until expiration. This phenomenon can have a significant impact on any number of trades you might consider.

In Figure 6.2 we saw that volatility on IBM options had ranged from as high as 55 to as low as 30. Table 6.5 shows the theoretical price for each call option if each option traded at a volatility of 55. Table 6.6 shows the theoretical price for each call option if each option traded at a volatility of 30.

To illustrate some of the dramatic differences between shorter-term and longer-term options, consider the February 90 call and the July 90 call. The February option has 39 days left

Table 6.5   IBM Theoretical Option Prices for Implied Volatility of 55

	Calls			
	JAN 11	FEB 39	APR 103	JUL 194
70	24.10	24.65	26.72	29.63
75	19.13	20.10	22.85	26.24
80	14.26	15.90	19.33	23.15
85	9.74	12.19	16.19	20.34
90	5.94	9.05	13.44	17.82
95	3.18	6.50	11.06	15.57
100	1.47	4.53	9.03	13.57
105	.59	3.06	7.32	11.80
110	.20	2.02	5.89	10.24
115	.06	1.29	4.72	8.88
120	.01	.81	3.76	7.69

Table 6.6   IBM Theoretical Option Prices for Implied Volatility of 30

	Calls			
	JAN 11	FEB 39	APR 103	JUL 194
70	24.10	24.37	25.10	26.38
75	19.11	19.42	20.43	22.07
80	14.12	14.58	16.05	18.11
85	9.17	10.07	12.14	14.57
90	4.64	6.26	8.80	11.48
95	1.56	3.44	6.12	8.88
100	.30	1.66	4.08	6.75
105	.03	.70	2.62	5.04
110	.00	.26	1.62	3.70
115	.00	.08	.96	2.68
120	.00	.02	.55	1.92

until expiration and the July option has 194 days. As you can see in Table 6.7, if volatility were to fall from 55 to 30—everything else being equal—the February 90 call would fall from a price of 9.05 to 6.26, a loss of 2.79 points or –30.8%. At the same time, the July 90 call would fall from a price of 17.82 to 11.48, causing a loss of 6.34 points or –35.6%. Table 6.8 shows how many points each option would lose if volatility fell from 55 to 30.

Table 6.7   Later-Dated Options Experience Larger Price Movements When Volatility Changes

Option	Price at 55 Volatility	Price at 30 Volatility	Points Lost If Volatility Falls from 55 to 30
February 90 Call	9.05	6.26	−2.79
July 90 Call	17.82	11.48	−6.39

Table 6.8   Raw Points Lost If Volatility Falls from 55 to 30

Strike	January	February	April	July
70	0.00	−0.28	−1.62	−3.25
75	−0.02	−0.68	−2.42	−4.17
80	−0.14	−1.32	−3.28	−5.04
85	−0.57	−2.12	−4.05	−5.84
90	−1.30	−2.79	−4.64	−6.34
95	−1.62	−3.06	−4.94	−6.69
100	−1.17	−2.87	−4.95	−6.82
105	−0.56	−2.36	−4.70	−6.76
110	−0.20	−1.76	−4.27	−6.54
115	−0.06	−1.21	−3.76	−6.20
120	−0.01	−0.79	−3.21	−5.77

Table 6.9   Percentage of Price Lost If Volatility Falls from 55 to 30

Strike	January	February	April	July
70	0.0%	−1.1%	−6.1%	−11.0%
75	−0.1%	−3.4%	−10.6%	−15.9%
80	−1.0%	−8.3%	−17.0%	−21.8%
85	−5.9%	−17.4%	−25.0%	−28.7%
90	−21.9%	−30.8%	−34.5%	−35.6%
95	−50.9%	−47.1%	−44.7%	−43.0%
100	−79.6%	−63.4%	−54.8%	−50.3%
105	−94.9%	−77.1%	−64.2%	−57.3%
110	−100.0%	−87.1%	−72.5%	−63.9%
115	−100.0%	−93.8%	−79.7%	−69.8%
120	−100.0%	−97.5%	−85.4%	−75.0%

The information presented in these tables has significant implications for both option writers and option buyers. For example, most option-writing strategies generally focus on writing short-term options in order to take advantage of time decay. However, if you are considering writing an option based primarily on an expected decline in volatility, you may actually get more value for your dollar by writing a longer-term option than a shorter-term one. Some traders buy long-term options so as to give themselves time for their trades to work out. Unfortunately, if they do not pay attention to volatility and inadvertently buy long-term options when volatility is high, they may sustain large losses if volatility falls, regardless of the action of the underlying security.

Summary

Option traders benefit from buying options when volatility is low because it means they are paying a lower price for the option than they would if volatility was high. This practice reduces the price they pay for the option, which reduces their break-even point and thus increases the probability of their earning a profit. By the same token, option writers benefit from writing options when volatility is high because it means they take in more premium, which in turn increases the probability that they will profit. Changes in volatility after a particular trade is entered can also have a profound effect on the potential for profit.

Traders who buy or write options without any regard to the current level of implied volatility or the effect that a significant change in volatility might have on their positions are essentially like a sailors at sea without a compass.

Chapter 7

PROBABILITY

At its core, option trading is a game of odds. Therefore, those who hope to be successful at trading options must focus on consistently placing the odds as much in their favor as possible on a trade-by-trade basis. Assessing the probability of profit or loss on a potential trade or group of trades can be another key factor in option-trading success. When you buy a stock (or go long a futures contract), the results depend entirely on whether or not that security rises or falls in price after it is purchased. However, with most option trades the expectations are not as straightforward. Because option prices include time premium—which will vanish by the time of option expiration—from a strictly mathematical point of view, an option buyer almost always has less than a 50% probability of profit, whereas the option writer generally has a greater than 50% probability of profit. The tradeoff is that while buyers of naked options enjoy the prospect of unlimited profit potential and limited risk, they also have a lower probability of profit. Conversely, writers of naked options enjoy a higher probability of profit but assume limited profit potential and unlimited risk.

Weighing the Pros and Cons

Although anyone can form an opinion in each case, the fact is that for any given option trade there is no way to state definitively whether the option buyer or option writer has the upper hand. The key point is not to theorize about who has the edge, but to

- Compare the risk and reward characteristics of several possible trades to determine which offers the most desirable trade-off between reward and risk.
- Simply be aware of the tradeoff being made. Too many traders buy naked options, believing in the unlimited-profit, limited-risk mantra, without realizing that they are entering into low-probability trades. Doing so consistently can doom them to failure. Other traders become enamored of the prospect of entering trades with a high probability of profit, which usually involves writing far-out-of-the-money options, without taking steps to minimize the attendant risk. This type of behavior is an invitation to disaster.

Even the casual option trader can benefit by learning to use probability as an aid by simply adopting the habit of always buying in-the-money options and writing out-of-the-money options. Another useful technique is to analyze the risk curves for a variety of possible trades in order to fully evaluate the relative risks and rewards associated with each position before making any trade.

Strategies for a Bullish Scenario

If a stock trader thinks a stock will advance in price, the choice is simple: Buy the stock. For the option trader there are myriad choices of potential trades. Each potential trade has its own unique risk and reward characteristics. Let's look at some examples that illustrate this point. Consider a situation in which a trader wants to profit from an expected rise in the price of a stock. We will consider three possible trading strategies to compare their advantages and disadvantages.

These are the three strategies we will consider:

1. Buy 100 shares of stock at a price of $94 a share.
2. Buy 1 February 90 call option at 9.88.
3. Write 10 February 75 put options at 1.375.

Figures 7.1 through 7.3 depict the expected profit or loss for each position through a range of prices from 64 to 124.

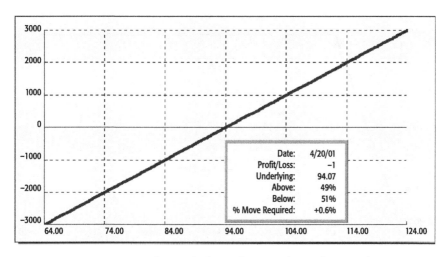

Figure 7.1   Risk curve for buying long 100 shares of IBM at 94.

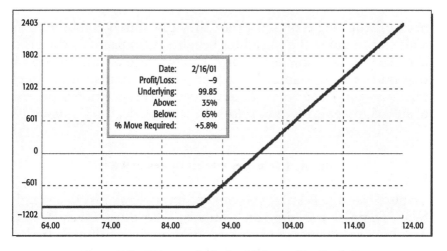

Figure 7.2   Risk curve for buying 1 February 90 call at 9.88.

Buying 100 Shares of Stock at 94

To purchase these shares traders must put up $9400 ($94 × 100 shares). One advantage of this position is that the traders actually own a piece of the company. They can hold the stock for as short or as long a time as they want. If they believe that the company

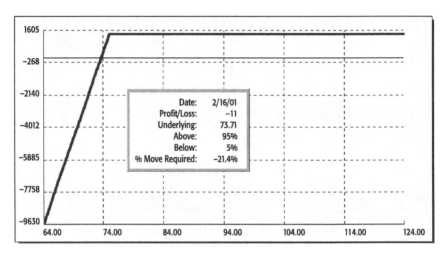

Figure 7.3   Risk curve for writing 10 February 75 puts at 1.375.

has brilliant long-term prospects, they can simply hold the stock
and wait to enjoy the hoped-for benefits. Compared to the other
choices in this example, the biggest advantage of this position is
that traders are guaranteed point-for-point movement if the stock
price goes up. The primary disadvantage of this position is the risk
of suffering a point-for-point loss if the stock declines in price.

Buying 1 February 90 Call Option at 9.88

To purchase one February 90 call option traders must invest only
$988, compared to the stock buyers, who must invest $9400.
The biggest advantage of this position is that although traders
put up only about one-tenth as much as buyers of 100 shares of
stock, they still enjoy the possibility of point-for-point movement with the stock above a price of 98.88. If the stock rises
strongly, they would enjoy a greater percentage rate of return
than would stock buyers. On the downside, they would lose
$988, or 100% of the investment, if IBM closes at 90 or lower at
the time of option expiration. Nevertheless, unlike stock traders,
who lose more money for every point the stock declines, they
can lose no more than the $988 they put up to enter the trade, re-
gardless of how far the stock may decline.

Writing 10 February 75 Put Options at 1.375

Writing put options is by far the most exotic of the three strategies. When buying stock or buying an option, traders put up the full amount of the purchase price in cash in order to enter the trade. When writing a naked option (which is the same as selling short an option), traders are required to put up margin. *Margin* is a good-faith deposit intended to guarantee that traders will meet their obligations if the option they have written is exercised against them. For naked options written on stocks, the formula for calculating margin requirements is 20% of the price of the stock minus the amount by which the option is out of the money. If this value is less than 10% of the price of the stock (times $100), traders must put up a minimum of 10% of the price of the stock (times $100).

The amount of margin required can fluctuate as the price of the stock rises or falls. If the stock begins to fall, naked option writers may be required to add more margin money to cover their margin requirement. Ultimately, writers of the naked put may be required to buy 100 shares of stock at the strike price for each option they have written. In the worst-case scenario for this trade, the writers would have to buy 100 shares of stock at $75 a share for each option contract assigned to them.

For this example, using the original margin requirement formula would result in a negative margin requirement, so the 10% rule applies. In other words, with IBM trading at 94, traders must put up $940 for every February 75 put option they want to write. Thus, to write 10 February 75 put options, traders must put up $9400 in margin money.

Original formula	(stock price × 20%) – (strike price – stock price)
	((94 × .20) – (75 – 94) × 100)
	((18.8 – 19) × 100) = –20
Minimum margin	(stock price × 10%) × 100
	(94 × 0.1) × 100 = $940
Margin on 10 contracts	$940 × 10 = $9400

The biggest advantage to this position is that traders can earn a profit even if the stock price falls significantly. The break-even price for this trade is 73.62 (equal to the strike price of 75 minus the premium collected of 1.375). In other words, if IBM stock falls to 75 at the time of February option expiration, the traders still get to keep the entire $1375 they collected when they wrote the options. Also, based on the historic volatility for IBM at the time of this trade, there is a 95% probability that IBM will be above the break-even price of 73.62 at the time of expiration. This high probability of profit is what draws many traders to writing options. Nevertheless, there are several negatives associated with writing naked options that must be carefully weighed before employing this strategy.

First, although the initial margin requirement to write one option ($940) is relatively low, the amount of margin money required would increase if the price of the stock began to fall. For example, if the stock fell to 80, the margin requirement for this position would rise to $1100 per contract. Also, should the price of the stock ultimately fall below 75, the traders would have to consider buying back the options—quite possibly at a significantly higher price—or the options may be exercised against them. If the options are exercised against the traders, the option writers are obligated to buy the 100 shares of stock at $75 a share. In other words, they would need $7500 per contract. A writer who is assigned on 10 option contracts would be required to buy $75,000 worth of stock (see Chapter 17 for a complete discussion of the strategy of writing naked puts). This represents a far different commitment than the initial margin requirement of $9400.

Profit/Loss Comparisons

Figures 7.1, and 7.2, and 7.3 depict the relative expectations associated with each of the three potential trades. Note that each of these trades will indeed make money if the stock rises. The variables are

- The amount of money required to enter each trade
- The dollar and percentage amount of profit to be obtained with each trade
- The worst-case scenario for each trade

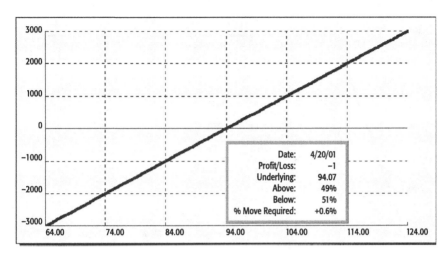

Figure 7.1   Risk curve for long buying 100 shares of IBM at 94.

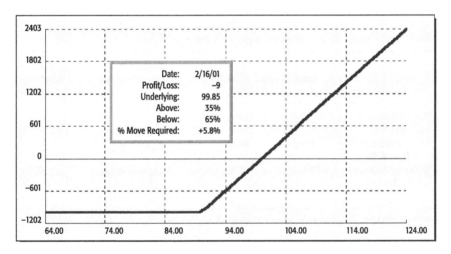

Figure 7.2   Risk curve for buying 1 February 90 call at 9.88.

Tables 7.1 and 7.2 depict the various entry considerations and expected returns over a range of stock prices for these three positions. If you were to ask 100 traders which of these three opportunities qualifies as the best trade, you would get a number of traders in each camp. The problem in this case—and with every new trade you consider—is not which is the best trade to make.

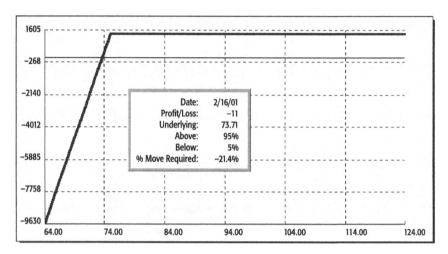

Figure 7.3   Risk curve for writing 10 February 75 puts at 1.37.

Table 7.1   Break-Even Analysis (Current Stock Price = 94)

Trade Entered	Initial Cost	Stock Break-Even Price	Probability of Percentage Move Required	Reaching Break-Even
Buy 100 shares at $94	$9400	94	0%	50%
Buy 1 February 90 call at 9.88	$988	98.88	+5.8%	35%
Write 10 February 75 puts at 1.375	$9400*	73.62	Anything better than a decline of –21.4% or more	95%

*Required margin may vary as stock price changes.

Table 7.2   Expected Returns Depending on Stock Price Movement

Trade Entered	Stock Down 30 Points	Stock Down 15 Points	Stock Unchanged	Stock Up 15 Points	Stock Up 30 Points
Buy 100 shares at $94	–$3000 (–32%)	–$1500 (–16%)	$0 0%	+$1500 +16%	+$3000 +32%
Buy 1 February 90 call at 9.88	–$988 (–100%)	–$988 (–100%)	–$488 (–49%)	+$913 +92%	+$2513 +154%
Write 10 February 75 puts at 1.375	–$11000 (NA)	+$1375 +15%	+$1375 +15%	+$1375 +15%	+$1375 +15%

The question that a trader needs to answer is "Which trade best fits my expectations and my risk tolerance constraints?" It is impossible to overstate the importance of giving yourself an honest answer each time out.

Delta

A value referred to as an option's delta can be calculated for each option by an option-pricing model. The delta value can range from 0 to 100 for calls and from 0 to –100 for puts. The significance of a particular option's delta value can be viewed in three ways:

1. The delta value for a given option provides an estimate of the probability that the option will expire in the money. Thus, an option with a delta of 20 currently has a roughly 20% probability of expiring in the money (although this is not mathematically correct, it does provide a useful estimate and a valuable frame of reference). This aspect of delta can be especially useful in assessing the probability of profit when comparing possible trades.
2. A delta value of 25 implies that if the underlying stock increases one full point, the option will increase in value by 0.25 point.
3. A delta value of 100 indicates that the option position is currently the equivalent of holding 100 shares of stock (or being long one futures contract). Thus, buying a put option with a delta of –40 means the position is presently equivalent to being short 40 shares of the underlying stock (or being short four-tenths of one futures contract). You should be aware that this is not a static value. The delta value for an option will change as time passes and as the underlying security's price rises or falls.

Table 7.3 displays the delta values for a series of call and put options for IBM on January 5 with the stock trading at $94. The further in the money a call option is, the higher its delta value. The further out of the money a call option is, the lower its delta value. This makes intuitive sense when you consider that the

Table 7.3   Deltas for IBM Call and Put Options

	Calls				Puts			
	JAN 14	FEB 42	APR 106	JUL 197	JAN 14	FEB 42	APR 106	JUL 197
70	99	95	89	86	–0	–4	–10	–13
75	96	90	84	81	–3	–9	–15	–18
80	90	83	78	76	–9	–16	–21	–23
85	80	74	71	70	–19	–25	–28	–29
90	66	63	63	64	–33	–36	–36	–35
95	49	52	55	58	–50	–47	–44	–41
100	34	42	48	52	–65	–57	–51	–47
105	21	32	41	47	–78	–67	–58	–52
110	12	24	34	41	–87	–75	–65	–58
115	6	17	28	36	–93	–82	–71	–63
120	3	12	23	32	–96	–87	–76	–67

further in the money a call option is, the greater the probability that it will expire in the money and the more price movement it will experience as the stock moves in price. Clearly, the February 80 call is more likely to expire in the money than the February 110 call. In addition, we would expect larger movements in price by the 80 call than the 110 call. These logical expectations are reflected by the fact that the February 80 call has a delta of 83 (suggesting an 83% probability of expiring in the money and suggesting that the option will rise 0.83 points if IBM rises one point in price), whereas the February 110 call has a delta of only 24 (suggesting a 24% probability of expiring in the money and suggesting that the option will rise 0.24 points if IBM rises one point in price).

Put option deltas work in the opposite manner. Put option deltas are negative because holding a long put option equates to being short the underlying security. The further in the money a put option is, the more negative its delta value. The further out of the money a put option is, the less negative its delta value. This makes intuitive sense when you consider that the further in the money a put option is, the greater the probability that it will expire in the money and the more price movement it will experience as the stock price moves. Clearly, the February 110 put is more likely to expire in the money than the February 80 put. In addition, we would expect larger movements in price by the 115 put than the 80 put. These logical expectations are reflected by the fact that the February 110 put has a delta of –75 (suggesting a 75% probability of expiring in the money and suggesting that the option will rise 0.75 points if IBM falls one point in price), whereas the February 80 call has a delta of only –16 (suggesting a 16% probability of expiring in the money and suggesting that the option will rise 0.16 points if IBM falls one point in price).

Traders often attempt to position trades so that they are *delta neutral*. This simply means putting on a combination of option positions so that when the positive and negative deltas are added together, the net result is as close to zero as possible. As long as a position is delta neutral, the price movement of the underlying security doesn't matter. Nevertheless, traders should be aware that option deltas change as the underlying market price moves. Thus, a trade that is delta neutral today may not be delta neutral tomorrow and may require a trader to either close the position, or rebalance the net position by closing out some positions or opening others to achieve delta neutrality once again.

Probability Analysis

It is possible to estimate the probability of profit for any given option trade by considering the volatility in price movement that a stock or futures contract has exhibited in the past. This information can be extremely useful when attempting to choose between more than one potential trade. For each option trade you can determine, or at least approximate, the break-even point. Using the historical volatility of the underlying security, you can then calculate the probability that the break-even price will be reached by some target date in the future. Let's look at an example to illustrate this concept.

Suppose a trader wanted to buy a straddle on Microsoft on January 5 with Microsoft trading at 49.12. For a trader willing to commit $3500 to a trade, here are two possibilities:

1. *February 50 straddle*
   Buy 4 February 50 calls at 4.25
   Buy 4 February 50 puts at 4.50

2. *February 55/45 straddle*
   Buy 7 February 55 calls at 2.31
   Buy 7 February 45 puts at 2.62

The risk curves for these two trades are shown in Figures 7.4 and 7.5. The key question for a trader is "Which trade should I make?" There are several factors to assess before an informed de-

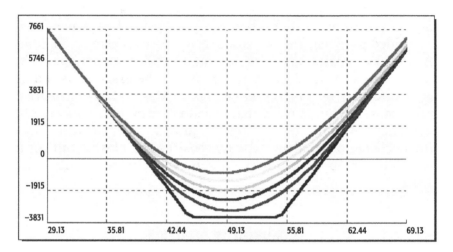

Figure 7.5   Risk curves for Microsoft 55 call/45 put straddle.

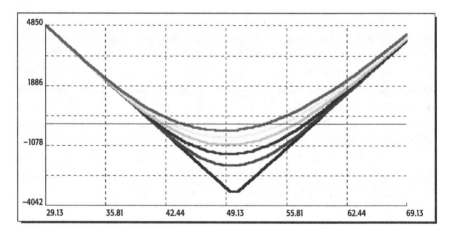

Figure 7.4   Risk curves for Microsoft 50 call/50 put straddle.

cision can be made; probability analysis can help in several areas. Consider the following:

- The distance between the current underlying price and the break-even points and the probability of closing outside these break-even points
- The expected return if the underlying stock makes a big move and the probability of actually achieving a big move
- The worst-case scenario and the probability of experiencing it

Figure 7.6 displays an analysis of probability for the 50 straddle. These are the key points:

- The 50 call/50 put spread costs $3500 to enter.
- The break-even points for this trade are 59.09 on the upside and 41.04 on the downside.
- With the stock at 49.12 and a historical volatility of 44.49, the probability of closing outside these break-even points at expiration is 22.71% (100% − 77.29%).
- A move of two standard deviations between January 5 and February option expiration would reach 63.89 on the upside or 34.36 on the downside.
- At 63.89 this trade would show a profit of $2056. At 34.36 this trade would show a profit of $2755.

		Probability Analysis	
Current Date	1/5/01	Current Price	49.12
Future Date	2/16/01	Upper Target:	59.09
Number of Days	42	Prob. Reach:	11.03%
Current Price	49.12	Prob. Not Reach:	88.97%
Volatility	44.49	Lower Target:	41.04
Upper Price Target	59.09	Prob. Reach:	11.68%
Lower Price Target	41.04	Prob. Not Reach:	88.32%
		Prob. of Closing between Targets:	77.29%

Figure 7.6 Probability of exceeding break-even prices at expiration for the Microsoft 50 straddle.

		Probability Analysis	
Current Date	1/5/01	Current Price	49.12
Future Date	2/16/01	Upper Target:	60.08
Number of Days	42	Prob. Reach:	9.10%
Current Price	49.12	Prob. Not Reach:	90.90%
Volatility	44.49	Lower Target:	39.81
Upper Price Target	60.08	Prob. Reach:	8.18%
Lower Price Target	39.81	Prob. Not Reach:	91.82%
		Prob. of Closing between Targets:	82.72%

Figure 7.7 Probability of exceeding break-even prices for the Microsoft 55/45 straddle at expiration.

Figure 7.7 shows an analysis of probability for the 55/45 straddle. These are the key points:

- The 55 call/45 put spread costs $3456 to enter.
- The break-even points for this trade are 60.08 on the upside and 39.81 on the downside.
- With the stock at 49.12 and a volatility of 44.49, the probability of closing outside these break-even points at expiration is 17.28% (100% – 82.72%) (see Figure 7.7).
- A two-standard deviation move between January 5 and February option expiration would reach 63.89 on the upside or 34.36 on the downside.
- At 63.89 this trade would show a profit of $2772. At 34.36 this trade would show a profit of $3996 (see Figure 7.7 and Table 7.4).

Table 7.4 illustrates the tradeoffs that must be considered when selecting trades to make—and it shows why there is a high rate of failure among option traders in general. It can be argued that traders should never consider entering a straddle unless they are highly confident that the underlying security will make a big move. In this example, if you truly expect Microsoft to make a big move in price, you should presumably buy the 55 call/45 put straddle, since that trade has the greatest profit potential. But consider the tradeoffs:

Table 7.4 Summary of Primary Considerations

Consideration	50 Straddle	55 Call/45 Put Straddle
Upside break-even point	59.04	60.08
Downside break-even point	41.04	39.81
Probability of being outside break-even points at expiration	22.7%	17.3%
2-standard-deviation up target	63.89	63.89
2-standard-deviation down target	34.36	34.36
Profit at 63.89 at expiration	$2056	$2772
Profit at 34.36 at expiration	$2755	$3996
Straddle experiences maximum loss if stock is between values at right	50	45 to 55
Probability of experiencing maximum loss	Less than 1%	49.2%

- The break-even points for the 55/45 straddle are further away than the break-even points for the 50 straddle, thus the 55/45 trade has a lower probability of profit.
- There is a far higher probability of sustaining a 100% loss while holding the 55/45 straddle until expiration than there is for the 50 straddle. The 50 straddle will sustain a 100% loss only if Microsoft is trading at exactly 50 at the time of February expiration. The 55/45 straddle will sustain a 100% loss if Microsoft is trading anywhere from 45 to 55 at the time of February expiration. At any price between 45 and 55, the 55/45 straddle will lose more money than the 50 straddle.

In sum, if a trader is going to trade straddles only occasionally, when he or she is highly confident that a big move is imminent, then a trade similar to the 55/45 straddle in this example makes sense because it offers the greatest potential return. Conversely, any trader who is planning to trade straddles on a regular basis might be better off using something like the 50 straddle in this example in order to minimize losses when the underlying security does not move as expected.

The Correct and Incorrect Ways to Use Probability

The primary mistakes traders make in assessing probability are

- Failing to assess the likelihood of making money before entering into a prospective trade
- Failing to manage their trades properly after they enter into them because they assume that the probabilities are on their side

Though it is hard to believe, it is a fact that most option traders have no idea what the probability is of making money on a particular trade when they enter into it. Consider that if you buy a call option with a delta of 33, you have only about a 1:3 chance of breaking even if you hold the option until expiration (this fact alone goes a long way toward explaining why speculators who only buy cheap, out-of-the-money options generally lose money in the long run).

On the other end of the spectrum, a trader may write a far-out-of-the-money call option with a delta of 10, realizing that this implies a 90% probability of making money (i.e., the option will expire out of the money and thus become worthless). This is a useful method for selecting options to write. The paradox, however, is that once this trade is entered, the proper question is no longer "What was my probability of making money when I entered the trade?" but "What am I going to do if the market moves sharply against me and I am faced with a loss?" If the underlying market rallies sharply, the trader in this example must act to cut losses, regardless of the initial probability of profit.

Following are the key points to remember about deltas and probability:

- You should assess the probability of profit *before* entering a trade.
- Do not put too much faith in the initial probability of profit once a trade is made. The probability of profit calculated when you enter a trade means nothing once you actually enter the trade. Once a trade is entered, it must be managed on the basis of dollars and cents, not probability.

Summary

For any given option trade it is possible to estimate the probability of profit or loss. An estimate is nothing more than an approximation, but this information can be extremely useful in helping a trader to choose between several potential trades. It can also be useful in assessing the trade off between reward and risk for any given trade.

As a simple tool, an option's delta value serves as a handy estimate of the likelihood that it will expire in the money. This information alone can often help astute traders to zero in on the specific option or options most likely to help them achieve their objectives. The historic volatility of the underlying security also can be used to estimate the likelihood that a given option trade will reach its breakeven point before option expiration. Information is power. Recognizing the likelihood of your success in advance is an area of analysis that far too many traders overlook.

Chapter 8

MARKET TIMING

As we have seen in previous chapters, many elements play important roles in your success or failure as an option trader. Another important factor is market timing. Depending on the type of option trading you do, timing can play a crucial role in your success. When you buy a stock or a futures contract, your timing must be reasonably good for you to make money. In other words, the price of the stock or futures contract must rise from its current level without first falling so far in price that you feel you must sell to cut your loss.

Probability, volatility, time until expiration, and volatility skew are important factors in the success or failure of trade, but the value of some strategies hinges primarily on accurate timing. Market timing has been the subject of thousands of books, articles, and videotapes. An exhaustive discussion of market timing is beyond the scope of this discussion, but we can touch on several option-trading situations in which timing plays a critical role. Some examples of each situation are provided to help you focus your attention in the right areas. These situations include the following:

- The underlying stock or futures contract is expected to move in a particular direction within a specific period.
- The underlying stock or futures contract is expected to trend in a particular direction without a specific time frame.
- The underlying stock or futures contract is expected to move significantly, but the direction is unknown.

- The underlying stock or futures contract is expected to stay in a particular range or at least not to move very far in any direction.

Options can be used to maximize your profitability given any of the preceding expectations. Two keys are

1. Being correct about your expectations
2. Using the proper trading strategy given your expectations and the current volatility level for the options on the underlying

Key 1 generally determines whether or not you will make money on your trade. Key 2 determines how much money you can make.

The Underlying Security Is Expected to Move within a Specific Period

If you are planning to buy naked calls and puts, it is crucial that you use a successful timing technique. If you buy calls and the underlying security falls in price or if you buy puts and the underlying security rises in price, you will invariably lose money. For traders who develop their own trading systems, one of the best tests you can run on a system for the purpose of buying naked calls and puts is to develop entry criteria and measure the price movement some number of days (x) later (testing different day windows as the variable x).

In other words, if you develop an entry criterion for buying calls and find that 70% of the time the underlying security is higher 5 days later, you have a very powerful tool for trading options. The criterion can be almost anything and the time frame can vary from one day to many months. With options, there are certain potential advantages associated with targeting a specific time frame.

The primary advantage of using a specific time frame is that it allows you to focus on a single strategy with certain expectations and without as much concern for factors you might otherwise have to consider. Let's look at an example. If you adopt a strategy that targets a 5-day time frame, such as buying a call option with the expectation of selling it within 5 trading days, you do not have the same concerns about changes in volatility and time decay as the trader who buys a call expecting a longer-term trend to develop.

If you are going to buy a naked call option with the idea of holding it for a month or more, you need to be very concerned with the level of implied volatility for that security when you enter the trade (see Chapter 6). If volatility is extremely high, you pay a lot more time premium than if volatility were low. Hence, you must be concerned about a decline in volatility, since such a decline would lower the price of all options on that security, including yours. In addition, you must be concerned about time decay since all the time premium you paid will decay as option expiration draws nearer.

If you buy an option with the intention of selling it within 5 days, you do not need to be quite as concerned about volatility and time decay. Certainly it is possible for volatility to fall significantly in a short period, but it is less likely to do so in the next 5 days than it is in the next month or more. Also, if you trade with a 5-day time frame, and as long as you don't buy options with less than a few weeks until expiration, you don't need to concern yourself as much with time decay. Although time premium on every option decays at least a small amount each day (see Chapter 5), the biggest effect is seen in the last few weeks before expiration.

On the other hand, the glaring disadvantage to trading with a particular time frame in mind is that the underlying security *must* make a move within your time frame or you will lose money. You also lose the opportunity to participate in major long-term trends.

Figure 8.1 depicts trading signals on the S&P 100 (OEX) stock index. (All figures in this chapter appear courtesy of Option Pro, Essex Trading Co., Ltd.) This system uses a moving average to determine the trend and then uses Welles Wilder's relative strength indicator to identify pullbacks against that trend in order to identify an entry signal. Finally, the trade is exited after either 7 trading days or an overbought reading (if holding calls) or

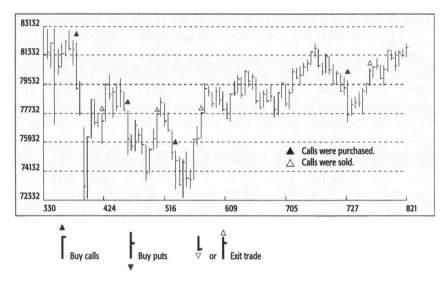

Figure 8.1   Example of short-term trading signals on the S&P 100 (OEX).

an oversold reading (if holding puts) from another momentum oscillator.

The Underlying Is Expected to Move in a Particular Direction but Not in a Specific Time Frame

Traders often decide that they expect a security to rise or fall, but they have no specific time frame in mind. Here, too, options can be used to maximize profitability, but other concerns specific to option trading must be taken into consideration.

Figure 8.2 depicts trading signals for Intel from a trend-following system. The system generates a buy-calls or buy-puts signal and holds that position indefinitely, depending on the action of the stock. As a result, a trade could conceivably last a day, a week, a month, or longer. However, there is no way to know at the time of the initial entry signal how long the trade will last. This has important implications for an option trader.

Option traders using a trend-following method such as this absolutely must take steps to minimize the amount of time

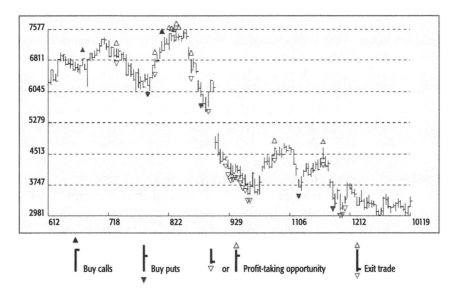

Figure 8.2   Trend-following trading signals on Intel.

decay their trades are exposed to. A trader trading without a specific time frame, who routinely buys expensive (i.e., high-volatility) options, will invariably lose money in the long run because time decay or declines in volatility, or both, will eventually eat away too much of the profit potential.

The Underlying Is Expected to Move Significantly but the Direction Is Unknown

One opportunity that is unique to option trading is the ability to enter a position that will create a profit whether the price of the underlying security rises or falls. The most common approach is to buy a straddle (see Chapter 15), which involves buying a call option and a put option simultaneously. The only reason to use this strategy is if you expect the underlying security to make a large price move and are not sure which direction it will move.

In general, stocks and futures markets tend to trend for a while and then consolidate for a while, then trend again, and so on. If you can identify a security that has been consolidating for a long time, you may surmise that it is likely to begin a new trend soon. If the only vehicle you have at your disposal is buying or selling short that stock or futures market, you must choose the direction you expect the anticipated trend to go. If you choose the right direction, you stand to make money; if you choose the wrong direction, you stand to lose money. In essence, you have a 50:50 chance of being right. Alternatively, instead of picking a direction, you can buy a call and a put simultaneously and wait for the underlying security to show a trend.

Figure 8.3 shows a proprietary oscillator that attempts to discern when a security is likely to trend, without giving any indication as to the direction of that trend. Whenever this oscillator exceeds 90 on the upside or 10 on the downside, it is suggesting that a trend may soon develop. Each such reading is marked on the chart by an up arrow and a down arrow. There are seven such signals on this chart for the underlying stock, America Online (AOL). Six of the seven signals were followed by price movements large enough to yield a profit to a trader who had bought a call and a put at the time of each signal.

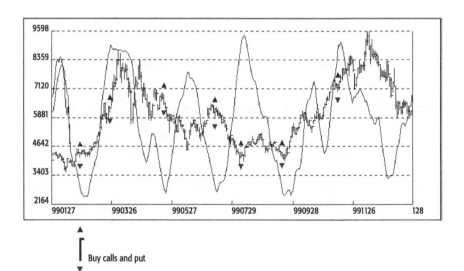

Figure 8.3 Nondirectional signals on America Online.

Traders can use a number of measures to identify quiet markets. Although a thorough discussion of the indicators is beyond the scope of this book, some examples that industrious traders may wish to explore are ADX, historical volatility ratios (e.g., the 6-day historical volatility divided by the 100-day historical volatility), and the number of trading days since the last x-day high or low.

The Underlying Is Expected to Stay within a Range or Not Move Much in Any Direction

One more opportunity unique to option trading is the potential to make money when a security does nothing. As discussed elsewhere in the book, there are a number of ways to take advantage of neutral situations, when a security displays no trend at all. Entry timing for these types of trades can be triggered by certain indicators, or more subjectively, by observing on a bar chart that a given security is presently bracketed by significant support and resistance levels.

Figure 8.4 shows several signals for Conseco (CNC) based on Welles Wilder's the ADX Directional Movement Index (DMI) indicator (on a scale of 0 to 100) exceeding the 75 level on the upside. These signals often indicate an overbought security that may be due for some consolidation. Overbought readings are noted by a solid down arrow. The overbought situation takes precedence over the ADX DMI indicator dropping below 50, which is shown by an empty down arrow.

Identifying overbought situations can be a very useful timing technique for investors who write covered calls. As you can see in Figure 8.4, between each solid arrow and each empty arrow the stock traded sideways to lower. A holder of Conseco stock could potentially have written out-of-the-money calls and collected premium as the stock trended lower.

Other strategies can be used to exploit this going-nowhere situation. They include buying calendar spreads, selling vertical spreads, selling naked puts, and entering butterfly spreads (see Chapters 14, 16, 17, and 19).

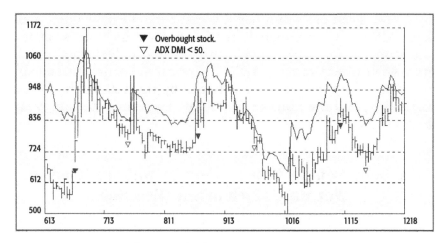

Figure 8.4 Covered call-writing opportunities for Conseco.

Summary

Market timing is essentially a quest for the holy grail. Sometimes a trader's timing is good, and sometimes it is not. Accurate timing when entering and exiting option trades can greatly increase your trading profits, and poor timing can generate large losses over time. The purpose of this chapter is not to reveal any mystical secrets of market timing but to start option traders thinking in terms of time frame and situation. Entirely different timing methods may be appropriate for a trader who is attempting to take advantage of a short-term move than for one who is trying to capture a long-term trend.

Chapter 9

TRADING REALITIES

Theory is one thing, reality is another. Nowhere is this truer than in the world of trading. At times it seems that there is a chasm a mile wide between theory and reality. In the real world of trading, all our well-thought-out trading plans, time-tested indicators, reliable patterns, and well-established relationships can suddenly stop working—completely and permanently—leaving a practitioner of these methods in danger of losing significant money. In a slightly less dire vein, often the simple day-to-day mechanics of trading can be different from what a trader expected them to be. This too can act as a serious impediment to long-term success. For example, if your method requires spending an hour a day updating data, analyzing markets, and placing orders, but you have only 30 minutes a day to devote to these tasks, then your approach has a fatal flaw that will likely cost you a lot of money.

This chapter discusses some realities of option trading that you should give some serious thought to. These can seem fairly mundane, but they can make a major difference in your trading.

Exercise and Assignment

If a call holder decides she wants to buy the underlying stock, or if a put holder decides he wants to sell the underlying stock, each would *exercise* his or her option. To do this, the buyer of an option indicates to her broker that she wants to exercise her option. Using something like a lottery process, some trader who is short that particular option would be *assigned* the obligation to deliver 100 shares of stock to the call option buyer. For example, say a trader is long one March call option with a strike price of 55. The stock rises to 65 and the trader decides she wants to own the stock. To make this happen she would call her broker and say that she wants to exercise this particular option. A trader who previously sold short the March 55 call and had not yet bought it back would be assigned on the option. This trader would need to either buy 100 shares of stock in the open market and deliver them to the option buyer (at a price of $55 per share) or deliver 100 shares of stock he already holds.

On the put side, consider a trader who is long one March put option with a strike price of 55. The stock falls to 45 and the trader decides he wants to short the stock from 55. To make this happen he calls his broker and says that he wants to exercise this particular option. A trader who previously sold short the March 55 put and has not yet bought it back would be assigned on the option. This trader would need to sell short 100 shares of stock in the open market and deliver them to the option buyer (for a price of $55 a share) or deliver 100 shares of stock she already holds short.

Another consideration often overlooked by novice traders is *automatic exercise*. When stock and stock index options expire, the Option Clearing Corporation automatically exercises any unclosed long call or put position that is at least one-eighth of a point in the money at the time of expiration. Because of this, in most cases, traders who are short an in-the-money option near expiration are best advised to close that position before expiration, unless they specifically want to hold a position, be it long or short, in the underlying security. Many a novice trader has been surprised on Monday morning after expiration to be holding a long or short position in the underlying.

Options can be either American style or European style. *American style* options can be exercised at any time up until option expiration. *European style* options can only be exercised at expiration. Most U.S. stock options are American style, and many stock index options are European style.

The Implications of Exercise

Though it does not get talked about much, the unexpected exercise of a short option position can have significant implications. Myriad spread strategies are available to an option trader. Some involve buying options at one strike price and selling options at another strike price. Traders often put on such trades after inspecting a risk curve that shows the expected profit or loss at expiration, thinking they will simply close out the trade at expiration with the indicated profit or loss. However, if the option (or options) they sold short as part of a spread were to trade deep in the money before expiration, there is a very real likelihood that the trades will be assigned on that option, forcing them to deliver stock while still holding the other options in their spread. This event can throw the expected results way out of whack.

Getting assigned on a short option is not a catastrophic event in and of itself. The important point is that the writer of an option must be aware of the possibility of getting assigned on that option and the potential impact of this event on the intended strategy.

When to Expect an Option to Be Exercised

There are two primary situations in which a trader can expect an option to be exercised. The first situation is at expiration. If you are holding a long option that does not settle in cash and you hold the position through expiration, you will end up with a long position in the underlying security. If you are short an option that does not settle in cash and you hold the position through expiration, you will end up with a short position in the underlying security.

You should also be concerned about being exercised on a short option if it is trading deep in the money. As a rule of thumb, if an option is trading at parity (i.e., there is no time premium in the price of the option) or just slightly above parity, you can generally expect it to be exercised.

An Example

One popular strategy for which option exercise is relevant is a backspread. Chapter 13 presents the various considerations for using a backspread. For now we focus solely on how early exercise can affect this trade. As an example of a backspread consider a position in which a trader sells one 50 call option at a price of 5 points and buys two 55 call options at a price of 2 points each. If the underlying stock rallies up to 70 or higher, the 50 call option that was written will be deep in the money. Once it loses almost all its time premium, the odds are great that the option will be exercised. Should this happen, the trader will have to either buy 100 shares of the underlying stock to deliver or buy back the option he has written. In either case he leaves himself with two long calls, which is not a position he intended to be in. If the stock price then falls, he stands to take serious losses as the long calls decline in price and he no longer has the short call position to offset some or all of those losses. His other alternative is to exercise one of his long calls. Should he choose this route, he would then be left with one long call option, which again is not the position he intended to be in when he entered into a backspread.

The question is not whether the trader in this example will ultimately make or lose money on this trade. The point of this example is to illustrate how the position he ended up with was far different from the one he intended to be in when he entered the trade. In the end he may make money, but not without first having to make some quick and unexpected decisions. What is important to understand is that the possibility for this type of situation exists whenever an option that you have written trades deep in the money.

Bid and Ask Prices and the Importance of Option Volume

When the time comes for new traders to move past the learning stage, after they have spent a lot of time absorbing the theory of options, the next step is to begin placing real orders, making real trades, and getting real fills. At this point many new traders experience something of a shock. When new traders test out their trading strategies, they often pull option prices out of the newspaper and assume that the price that appears in the newspaper was the price at which they bought or sold. In fact, many new traders make the mistaken assumption that if a price is printed in the paper they can buy or sell as many options as they want to at that price. This is not true.

When you place an order to buy (or sell) a given option, you can obtain the latest bid and ask price quotes, either from your broker or from a data service. If you place a *market* order to buy an option (i.e., you want to buy the option without specifying a price), you pay the ask price. If you place a market order to sell an option (i.e., you want to sell the option without specifying a price), you receive the bid price.

The effect of buying at the ask price and selling at the bid price can have a profound effect on your trading results, both on a trade-by-trade basis and cumulatively.

Appreciating the Effect of Bid-Ask Spreads

Table 9.1 displays option price information for IBM on January 5. The grid shows the last trade price ("Market") as well as the current bid and ask prices for each option. Careful study of this grid will help you to obtain a sense of what to expect in the real world.

To gain a true appreciation of the effect that bid-ask spreads have in real-world trading, consider the following example. Say you are bullish on IBM stock and decide to buy 10 contracts of the February 100 call option at the current market price. The current asked price is 4.88, so you pay $4875 to buy the 10 contracts (4.875 × $100 × 10 contracts). Moments later you get buyer's remorse, deciding that you have made a bad trade and you want to exit the trade immediately. The stock is still trading at the same price, so you place a market order to sell your 10 option contracts. Because nothing has changed in those few seconds between the time you bought the options and the time that your order to sell these options hits the market, you might expect to

Table 9.1 IBM Option Bid and Asked Prices

Strike		Calls				Puts			
		JAN 14	FEB 42	APR 106	JUL 197	JAN 14	FEB 42	APR 106	JUL 197
80	Market	15.25	16.50	19.75	21.50	1.38	2.38	4.25	5.62
	Bid	15.25	16.50	19.25	21.50	1.19	2.19	4.00	5.62
	Asked	15.75	17.00	19.75	22.25	1.38	2.44	4.38	6.12
85	Market	11.12	13.00	15.75	18.50	2.06	3.62	5.88	7.38
	Bid	11.12	12.75	15.75	18.50	1.94	3.38	5.62	7.38
	Asked	11.62	13.25	16.25	19.00	2.12	3.62	6.00	7.88
90	Market	7.88	9.50	13.12	15.75	3.50	5.12	7.88	9.88
	Bid	7.50	9.50	12.75	15.75	3.25	5.12	7.50	9.38
	Asked	7.88	9.88	13.25	16.25	3.50	5.50	7.88	9.88
95	Market	4.50	6.88	10.12	13.25	5.25	7.62	10.12	12.00
	Bid	4.38	6.75	10.12	13.00	5.25	7.38	9.75	11.62
	Asked	4.75	7.12	10.62	13.50	5.62	7.75	10.12	12.12
100	Market	2.38	4.75	8.00	10.88	8.12	10.12	12.50	14.38
	Bid	2.38	4.50	7.88	10.88	8.12	10.12	12.50	14.25
	Asked	2.62	4.88	8.25	11.38	8.50	10.62	13.00	14.75
105	Market	1.31	3.00	6.12	8.88	12.50	13.38	16.25	17.38
	Bid	1.12	3.00	6.12	8.88	12.00	13.38	15.75	17.38
	Asked	1.38	3.25	6.50	9.38	12.50	13.88	16.25	17.88
110	Market	.62	2.00	4.88	7.50	17.00	17.75	19.12	20.62
	Bid	.62	1.81	4.62	7.38	16.50	17.25	19.12	20.62
	Asked	.75	2.06	5.00	7.88	17.00	17.75	19.62	21.38
115	Market	.31	1.25	3.50	6.12	21.62	21.38	23.00	24.38
	Bid	.25	1.00	3.50	6.00	20.88	21.38	22.88	24.38
	Asked	.38	1.25	3.75	6.50	21.62	22.12	23.62	25.12
120	Market	.12	.56	2.62	4.75	25.75	25.88	27.00	28.25
	Bid	.12	.56	2.62	4.75	25.75	25.88	27.00	28.25
	Asked	.19	.75	2.88	5.12	26.50	26.62	27.75	29.00

break even on the trade. But you won't—not even close. The contracts will be sold at the latest bid price of 4.50 and you will collect proceeds of $4500 (4.50 × $100 × 10 contracts). In sum, even excluding commissions, you lose $375 on this trade, or 7.7% of your initial $4875 investment.

The bottom line is this: Make no mistake about the importance of considering the effect of bid-ask spreads on your trading.

Factors in Dealing with Bid-Ask Spreads

Generally speaking, you can expect to find the bid-ask spreads for stock and stock index options, as seen in Table 9.2.

At times, trading in the face of the bid-ask spread can seem like playing against a stacked deck—and in some ways it is. Nevertheless, this is the reality of the situation. If you want to trade options, you must deal with bid-ask spreads, and often you will find them wider than you would like them to be. Your alternatives are to trade, not trade, or use *limit orders*.

A Word on Limit Orders

An old maxim in option trading is "Get in at your price, get out at the market." These few words contain much useful wisdom. Essentially what it is saying is, "Be particular about entering trades, and don't linger too long when it's time to go." Traders may get a market-timing idea and decide to enter an option trade without much regard for the price of purchasing the option. On a given trade this can work out alright if the trader's timing is good enough and the underlying security makes a large move in

Table 9.2 Typical Bid-Ask Spreads on Stock and Index Options

Price of Option	Usual Bid-Ask Spread
Options trading under 1.00	0.0625 to 0.25
1.00 to 10.00	0.25 to 0.375
Over 10.00	0.375 to 1.00

the right direction. However, disregard for the price being paid can take a very high toll in the long run.

One alternative is to use a limit order. A *limit order* is an order that ensures that you won't pay more than a price you specify to purchase a particular option or receive less than a price you specify to sell an option. For example, say a trader wants to buy the IBM February 95 call option shown in Table 9.1. The current ask price in this example is 7.12. A trader has two choices. She can pay 7.12 ($712.50 per contract) and enter the trade immediately, or she can place a limit order to buy the option at a lower price. For example, she could call her broker and say, "I want to buy 10 IBM February 95 calls at 6.88 limit good-till-canceled." By placing this order the trader is saying that until further notice (i.e., until she either cancels the order or until February option expiration), if the option can be bought at 6.88, she will buy the option. In this case, if her order does eventually get filled on a 10-lots, she will have saved herself $250 (7.125 – 6.875 × 10-lot × 100 = $250) compared to what she'd have paid if she'd placed a market order.

The biggest danger in using a limit order is that you run the risk of missing a trade altogether. Consider the previous example. Suppose the trader's timing was exactly right and the price of IBM stock began to rise immediately. The option might have rallied from 7.12 to 14.25. By placing a market order to buy 10 calls, the trader would have bought her 10 options at 7.12 and could have doubled her money. Conversely, by placing a limit order to buy at 6.88, the trader would have missed the move completely because the option did not get back down to her limit price.

On the flip side, say another trader wants to enter a long calls position on the next open. One choice would be to place an order to buy the calls *market on open*. This means that he would buy the calls at whatever the opening price of the day happens to be. The danger in this situation is that the underlying stock or futures market could gap open substantially higher in price, thus inflating the price of the call options and greatly increasing the amount the trader pays to buy the calls. For example, suppose that based on the previous day's closing prices, a trader thinks that 7.00 is a good price to pay for the IBM February 95 calls, with IBM having closed at a price of 100. The trader places an order to buy 10 95 calls market on open. Unexpectedly, IBM stock gaps open 10 points higher and the open price for the 95 calls is 17.00. Thus the trader ends up paying $17,000 to buy the calls rather than the $7000 he expected to pay. The stock then sells off, and the price of the call option falls all the way back to 7.00, resulting in a loss of $10,000. In this case, the trader could have saved himself a great deal of money by placing an order to buy 10 calls at a limit price of 7.00 per contract. Had he done so in this case, no position would have been entered until the price of the option fell back to the limit price of 7.00 per contract.

There is no one right or wrong answer to the question of whether to use a limit order in a given situation. That is why this chapter is called "Trading Realities." The guiding principle should generally be based on

- *Your own risk/reward profile.* Some traders routinely use options to "take a shot" and try to maximize their profitability on a given market call. When betting on long shots, the important task is to understand the downside risk on both a trade-by-trade basis and on a cumulative basis.
- *The probability of profit on each trade, depending on the price paid.* Here is where learning to assess the implications for a risk curve for a given trade can be extremely useful. In the end it doesn't really matter whether you are buying a call, selling a put, or entering a spread. What matters is what the underlying security must do so that you can earn a profit, and the downside risk of the trade.
- *The confidence you have in your outlook for a given trade.* If you expect a particular price movement and expect it to start right now, you have no reason to use a limit order. If your sole intention is to participate in an expected move that you are highly confident is imminent, you should eschew limit orders and simply enter at the market. In this case, if you are right, the use of a limit order may cause you to miss the move completely.

Summary

Many individuals enter the real world of trading unprepared for the harsh realities that await them. Within the realm of option trading it is important for traders to understand the effect that exercise and assignment can have on certain positions they might enter. A carefully crafted spread position can be thrown completely out of whack when the trader is assigned on a short option. To be successful, a trader must understand that this possibility exists and under what circumstances it is most likely to occur.

Traders must also acknowledge and deal with the spreads between bid and ask prices. This is extremely important when trading options because this spread can often represent a large percentage of the option price. A given stock last traded at 50.10 may currently be trading at 50 bid, 50.20 asked. This spread represents only four-tenths of 1% of the current stock price. On the other hand, an option last traded at 2.50 may currently be trading at 2.30 bid, 2.70 asked. This spread represents 16% of the current option price. The size of this spread can have a profound impact not only on each individual trade but also on a trader's long-term success or failure.

In general, traders are better off if they enter a trading campaign with realistic expectations and a clear understanding that some factors exist that will almost invariably work to their disadvantage. All traders who are successful in the long run share a certain degree of mental toughness that allows them to overcome adversity.

Chapter 10

IMPORTANT CONCEPTS TO REMEMBER

An option trader must understand several key concepts if he or she hopes to succeed in the long run. This chapter summarizes these ideas, which are discussed in greater detail in previous chapters. The examples in the previous chapters hold the keys to a full understanding of each concept. Once you begin to learn the ideas, this chapter will serve as a one-stop reference guide to them. This chapter also establishes a framework for selecting trades using these important concepts as a guide.

Valid Reasons to Trade Options

As discussed in Chapter 2, several opportunities might prompt someone to trade options. Options offer a variety of unique opportunities that are not available to individuals who only buy (and sell short) underlying securities such as stocks and futures. The primary opportunities are

- The ability to gain leverage when betting on price direction
- The ability to hedge an existing position in a given underlying security
- The ability to take advantage of neutral situations (i.e., in which the underlying security stays in a narrow price range)

These are all viable investment objectives, and each represents a trading opportunity unique to option traders. There is no way to take advantage of neutral situations by buying or selling short stocks or futures contracts. The only way to make money when an underlying security is going nowhere is with options. Since most securities trend for only short periods, learning to take advantage of neutral strategies makes a great deal of sense.

Option Pricing

As discussed in Chapter 4, options are a derivative security, that is, they trade based on the price movements of some other underlying security. As such, a method is needed to determine a fair price for any option. The most commonly used method is an option-pricing model. The most widely used one is the Black-Scholes model. After variables are entered, including the underlying price, the strike price of a given option, the number of days left until expiration, and a volatility value, an option-pricing model calculates a theoretical price for the option, also known as fair value. This value gives traders some idea of what price they should reasonably expect to pay to buy a given option or how much they should reasonably expect to receive from writing a given option. As with any other commodity, particularly an investment, it is critically important not to overpay when buying an option nor to be underpaid when selling. An understanding of option models and theoretical option pricing gives the trader the proper frame of reference for analyzing any potential option trade.

Time Decay

As discussed in Chapter 5, until traders fully understand and appreciate the effect of time decay, they are unlikely to be consistently successful. The reason for this is that the time premium built into any option price will decay to zero by the time of option expiration. This has an inevitable effect on all options and virtually all option positions. Whatever time premium is built into the price of an option will ultimately evaporate. Therefore, it is critical for an option buyer to take steps to minimize the negative effects of time decay and for an option writer to maximize the potential benefits of time decay. The methods of using time decay to your advantage are discussed in more detail in the upcoming strategy chapters.

Volatility

If time decay is the enemy of all option buyers, then monitoring volatility is the most useful tool in allowing traders to determine whether they are paying a little or a lot in terms of time premium. As discussed in Chapter 6, volatility is a key input factor when determining the fair value of a given option. The higher the level of volatility, the higher the option prices are for a given security. Conversely, the lower the volatility level, the lower the option prices are for a given security. In essence, the current level of implied volatility tells you whether an option (or a series of options on a given security) is cheap, expensive, or somewhere in between. This information has significant implications for the option trader.

If implied option volatility for a given security is very high,

- You can be certain that you will pay more time premium if you buy an option than you would if volatility were low
- If volatility falls before expiration, time premium levels may fall significantly, even beyond the normal amount of time decay

If implied option volatility for a given security is very low,

- You can be certain that you will receive less time premium if you choose to write an option than you would if you did so when volatility was high
- If volatility rises before expiration, time premium levels may rise significantly

Finally, regardless of the current level of volatility, whatever time premium exists in the price of an option will evaporate by option expiration.

Trading without this knowledge is like buying a used car without checking the blue book value first—you would have no frame of reference for reasonably determining if you are paying too little or too much for the item you are planning to buy.

Probability

As discussed in Chapter 7, in option trading it is possible to ascertain which of several potential trades offers the highest probability of generating a profit. Doing such analysis is almost always time well spent. Nevertheless, as with all aspects of option trading, there are tradeoffs here, too. For example, if you buy a deep-in-the-money call option, you have a much greater probability of profit than if you buy a far-out-of-the-money option. However, if the underlying security makes a huge move in the anticipated direction, you stand to make a lot less money than you would if you bought the far-out-of-the-money option because the out-of-the-money option offers greater leverage. In the end, probability analysis allows traders to determine which of any number of potential trades they are most comfortable with, given their own preferences for reward and risk.

Market Timing

Market timing is the wild card in option trading. Depending on the position you enter, your timing must be near perfect, must be fairly accurate, or is only slightly relevant. Make no mistake about it, the better your timing, the more likely you are to make money trading options. However, many traders tend to overrate their own market-timing ability, which means their expectations of profit are greater in their own minds than they are in reality. One way around this problem is to use neutral strategies, such as buying straddles and calendar spreads, which do not require accurate forecasts of the future direction of the underlying security. For traders who are so inclined, time spent identifying entry criteria that have a high probability of generating a price movement in the predicted direction over a fixed period can be time well spent.

How to Lose Money Trading Options

Without a doubt, the easiest thing to do in option trading is lose money. Because you either pay a premium on top of any real (or *intrinsic*) value that an option may have when you buy an option, or you assume limited profit potential and possibly unlimited risk when writing an option, you are generally faced with either a low probability of profit or an unfavorable reward-to-risk potential. These are potentially serious impediments to profitability. Therefore, identifying the reasons that most losing traders fail is an important first step in avoiding these potential pitfalls.

Never Do Anything but Buy Low-Priced, Out-of-the-Money Options

Probably the number 1 trap most unsuccessful option traders fall into is that of regularly buying low-priced or far-out-of-the-money options. Most people believe that cheaper means a better deal. This is definitely untrue when it comes to buying far-out-of-the-money options. The common phrase, "You get what you pay for," generally applies here. Buying a far-out-of-the-money option almost always amounts to a long-shot bet. As with most long-shot bets, the odds are almost always very much against you when you place the bet (or in this case, enter the trade). As with the bettor who always bets on the long-shot horse to win, there may be some memorable winners along the way, but the odds of achieving lasting success via this approach are overwhelmingly long. Placing low-probability bets trade after trade is no way to achieve long-term success. The way to avoid this trap is to analyze the probability of making money on each trade and to avoid habitually entering trades that have an extremely low probability of profit.

Pay No Attention to Time Premium Levels and Time Decay

The material in Chapters 5 through 7 demonstrates the importance of time premium and the necessity for traders to assess the amount of time premium they are paying to minimize the negative effect it might have on their trades. Traders who pay no attention to time premium levels are generally doomed to failure for the simple reason that they are going from trade to trade without ever bothering to consider whether the prices they pay for the options they buy are too high (or if the prices they receive for the options they write are too low). Novice traders are also easily lured into buying options with little time left until expiration, again succumbing to the misconception that low-priced options represent some type of bargain. As illustrated in Chapter 5, time decay accelerates as option expiration draws nearer. This fact alone makes short-term options a dangerous bet, particularly if the bulk of your trading involves buying these options.

These mistakes are common among traders who focus solely on market timing and who think their timing is so good that time decay won't be a factor. This leads us to another common cause of failure among option traders.

Assume That Your Market Timing Is Good Enough to Overcome All

As mentioned earlier in this chapter, market timing is a wild card in option trading. If you are a great market timer, you can reasonably expect to make a good deal of money trading options. Nevertheless, it is foolish to overlook the other factors that can work against you, trade in and trade out. When you buy a call option on a stock, not only must the stock price rise for you to make money, it also must rise far enough and fast enough to offset the negative effect of time decay. A small rise in the price of the stock may make a winner out of the buyer of the stock itself, but it may not necessarily result in a profit for the buyer of an option on that stock. Traders who dismiss this subtlety of option trading severely hurt their chances for success.

Try to Follow the Options on Every Single Stock or Futures Market

It is a common desire of many traders to be able to scan the universe of available options in an effort to find the best trade. This is an understandable desire. The thinking goes like this: "If I consider every possible option, I am sure to find the best trade." In some cases this may be a reasonable goal. For instance, if you are looking for certain types of spread opportunities, it can make sense to cast as wide a net as possible. Unfortunately, too many traders who set out to scan the universe of options do not have a clear enough idea of what it is they are really looking for. Also, for the majority of traders, the effort required to scan the universe is often not worth the results they achieve.

First, consider that even with a computer, scanning all available options is a very time-consuming process. Second, if you are looking for a truly unique opportunity, odds are you will not find it every day. Thus, you may end up spending a great deal of time scanning and very little time actually finding good trades, which eventually leads to frustration and the abandonment of this approach. The bottom line is this: There is nothing wrong with scanning a large number of securities if you are looking for something specific. However, under most circumstances your time is generally better spent narrowing your focus before performing any scan.

For instance, you might first compile a list of stocks whose options are currently trading near the low end of their historical range of implied volatility and then consider evaluating option-buying strategies with these stocks. Conversely, you might instead compile a list of stocks whose options are currently trading near the high end of their historical range of implied volatility and then consider evaluating option-writing strategies. This type of approach can save a tremendous amount of time and can be expected to yield more useful results than trying to consider every single available option.

Take Great Comfort in Knowing That All You Can Lose Is Everything You Put Up

Many option traders are essentially hypnotized by the limited-risk, unlimited-profit-potential mantra associated with options. On one hand, the statement is entirely true. If you buy a call or a put option, the most you can lose is whatever you pay to buy the option. This is true no matter how far the underlying stock or futures contract may move in the wrong direction—and it is an attractive feature. Nevertheless, several sobering realities must also be considered. First, if you buy an option, you do have unlimited profit potential if the underlying security makes a big move. However, in most cases, within a certain range of prices above and below the current underlying price, you likely have greater downside risk than you do upside potential. This is because you are paying time premium on top of intrinsic value to buy a given option. Consider the following example.

On January 5, with IBM trading at 94, you buy one IBM February 95 call for 7.12 ($712.50). As illustrated in Figure 10.1, if the stock rises 6 points in two weeks, this trade will show an open profit of approximately $183. If, however, the stock falls 6 points in two weeks, this trade will show an open loss of $425. In other words, although the trade technically enjoys the prospects of limited risk and unlimited potential, in the short term, over a certain range of prices, the trade will show a greater loss on the downside than it will a profit on the upside. This is a far cry from the limited-risk, unlimited-profit-potential nirvana that many option traders anticipate. Additionally, if you hold this option until expiration and IBM is trading at or below 95, you will lose the full $712 you invested. Although that may be some consolation if you had considered buying the stock and the stock happened to collapse, the fact remains that you lost

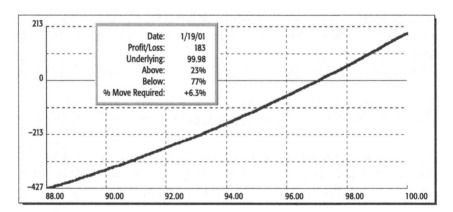

Figure 10.1 Expected return on IBM February 95 call.

your entire investment on the trade. Moral victories are important from time to time, but you can't take them to the bank.

The Keys to Success in Option Trading

There are certain concepts a trader must understand to be successful trading options. Although traders can enjoy success using widely varying approaches, certain guidelines must be adhered to, regardless of the approach you use. The key trading guidelines are

- Understanding the strategies available
- Knowing when to employ a given strategy for maximum benefit
- Accurately assessing the current level of volatility
- Knowing whether the time is right to buy premium or sell premium
- Knowing when to take advantage of disparities in the implied volatilities of different options
- Buying undervalued options and selling overvalued options
- Knowing when to take a profit
- Knowing when to cut a loss

By now you should be getting some idea of what it takes to succeed as an option trader. Now that we have detailed some of the mistakes to avoid, let's learn the key habits you must adopt to achieve long-term success.

Buy Options Composed Mostly of Intrinsic Value

By now you should understand that time decay is the enemy of all option buyers. The most effective way to minimize the negative effect of time decay on the options you buy is simply not to pay much time premium in the first place. The easiest way to achieve this goal consistently is to get into the habit of buying options whose price contains little time premium, which almost always involves buying in-the-money options. This goes against the grain for many traders who think they are trying to maximize their profitability and therefore gravitate to the least expensive options that offer the greatest leverage. This is a key point: The further out of the money the option, the greater the leverage and the lower the probability of profit. Too many traders focus on the leverage aspect of options and forget to consider the probability aspect. Traders who have been around for a while and have had some success in buying options come to learn that buying in-the-money options is one of the secrets to option-buying success.

The negatives to buying in-the-money options are that they cost more to buy and they offer less leverage. If the underlying stock or futures contract makes a huge move in the anticipated direction, the fact is that you simply will not get the same profit you would by buying a far-out-of-the-money option. However, although these negatives are real, buying an in-the-money option gives you a greater probability of profit and allows you the quickest chance to achieve point-for-point profit with the underlying security. Buying a far-out-of-the-money option may give you leverage of 50:1, whereas an in-the-money option may only give you leverage of 10:1. The factor most easily missed in looking at leverage is probability. If the 50:1 bet has a 5% probability of profit and the 10:1 bet has a 50% probability of profit, the 10:1 leverage trade is a better bet.

Write Options Made Up Mostly (or Completely) of Time Premium

Time decay is inevitable, and any and all time premium built into the price of an option will evaporate by the time of expiration. This factor does inarguably work in favor of the option writer. Writing a naked option entails assuming unlimited risk and may not be suitable for many traders. Nevertheless, writing out-of-the-money options is as close to a free lunch as you are likely to find in the investment world. If you write an out-of-the-money option when volatility levels are high, you put several powerful forces to work for you.

- By virtue of writing an out-of-the-money option, you are selling a wasting asset, which—barring a change in the price of the underlying—is guaranteed to lose all its value by expiration. Granted, the underlying could move far enough to force the option to trade in the money, but this is a known risk. In any event, by writing an out-of-the-money option, you establish a position that, mathematically speaking, has a better than 50% probability of earning a profit.

• By focusing your option writing on situations in which implied volatility is high, you can maximize the amount of time premium you collect. Similarly, if volatility collapses after you write an option, the price of the option you wrote will also collapse, often giving you an opportunity to take an early profit rather than having to wait until option expiration.

Identify a Handful of Trading Strategies You Can Be Comfortable Using in Various Situations

For traders to be consistently successful, they must have a clear idea of the potential rewards and risks associated with the type of trading they are doing. Nowhere is this truer than in option trading.

An almost countless number of option trading strategies are available (several of the more useful ones are detailed in the following chapters). Although this variety provides flexibility, which is essentially a plus, the problem is that traders often end up dabbling in a variety of trading strategies because they look interesting. More often than not, however, traders fail to fully understand the associated risks and rewards before using the strategy and eventually lose enough money that they decide not to use that strategy anymore.

The key is to take the time to learn the pros and cons of each option-trading strategy and the unique opportunity each strategy offers. Some strategies are best used to take advantage of high volatility or low volatility, but naïve traders inadvertently use these strategies at the wrong time and end up with little chance of making money. For example, a trader may buy options when volatility is extremely high. Volatility then collapses and the price of the trader's option also collapses, leaving little chance of profit. In addition, some strategies are best used when you are extremely bullish or bearish, and others are designed to take advantage of neutral situations. Without a clear understanding of which strategy is designed to achieve which objective, the odds of making a mistake are great. The material presented in Chapters 12 through 19 gives you an understanding of how and when to use each of these strategies.

Focus Your Attention Primarily on Stocks with Active Option Volume

The benefit you gain by dealing in actively traded options is liquidity. Generally speaking, the more actively traded the option, the tighter the bid-ask spread, and the more closely the option will trade to fair value. The upshot is that the more actively traded the option, the more likely you are to be able to buy or sell it at a favorable price. This concept escapes most new traders until they lose enough money due to wide bid-ask spreads on illiquid options to cause them to change their thinking. There is nothing wrong per se with trading thinly traded options as long as you understand the implications of this spread on your trades and are willing to assume that risk.

Summary

- Develop a plan for trading options:
  - What strategies will I use?
  - What criteria will I use to enter a trade?
  - What criteria will I use to exit with a profit?
  - What criteria will I use to exit with a loss?

- Once you have a plan, which includes risk control measures, follow that plan.
- Focus the bulk of your attention on securities that have active option volume.
- If volatility is low, focus on buying premium.
- If volatility is high, focus on selling premium.
- Buy options with little time premium.
- Write options that are all time premium.
- Before entering any trade, determine how much of an effect time decay will have on your position.

- Before entering any trade, determine your probability of profit. If it is low, trade smaller or skip the trade altogether.
- Before entering a trade, make sure the bid-ask spread is reasonable. When you want to exit the trade, look for consistently good volume to ensure a reasonable bid-ask spread.
- Use a timing method with as high a winning percentage as possible.
- When buying naked options, buy in-the-money options (to reduce the negative effect of time decay).
- If volatility is high, skip naked call buying and use another strategy.
- Don't write calls against your entire stock position (this limits your upside potential—see Chapter 18).

Chapter 11

OVERVIEW OF TRADING STRATEGY GUIDES

In the long run, no one makes money trading options by being lucky. If you hope to succeed over time, you must understand what it takes to succeed and apply those key principles consistently. So far we have discussed the most important concepts associated with successful option trading. Another key element in trading success is knowing which trading strategy to apply in a given situation. Many option traders are one-trick ponies: They either buy calls and puts, or they write covered calls, or they employ some other pet strategy, and this amounts to the sum total of their option-trading knowledge. This is unfortunate, given the myriad possibilities available to the savvy trader. The trader who can examine a situation and decide which strategy will maximize the opportunity is the trader who stands the greatest chance of real success in the long run.

The Two Key Elements in Selecting a Trading Strategy

Appendix A contains an outline of my PROVEST Option Trading Method, which incorporates five key elements to aid in trade selection. In the following chapters on strategy, all the relevant criteria for a given strategy are discussed. For now, however, our goal is to simplify the option-trading process. When you boil it all down, there are two key elements that a trader must consider when choosing the proper trading strategy for a given situation. One of those elements is volatility. As discussed in detail, volatility is an extremely important consideration because the level of volatility for a security at a particular point in time tells you whether the options on that security are cheap, expensive, or somewhere in between. With this information, you will be able to decide whether you are better off buying premium or selling premium at this moment.

The other key element is a trader's own opinion on price direction. When assessing the option trading possibilities for a given security, you must decide if you want to pursue a directional strategy or a neutral strategy. If you are definitely bullish or bearish on a given security, you will want to pursue a directional strategy. You can then look at volatility for a clue as to whether you should be buying or writing options. Conversely, there may be times when you expect a given security to remain within a particular price range for some period, and thus may decide to pursue a neutral trading strategy. Again, volatility provides the clue as to whether option buying or option writing is the best course of action.

Table 11.1 and the information presented in Chapters 12 through 19 are designed to help traders decide which strategy to use and how best to execute the strategy.

Table 11.1 Trading Strategy Matrix

	Low Volatility	High Volatility
Directional bias	Buy a naked call or put (Chapter 12)	Sell a vertical spread (Chapter 16)
	Buy a backspread (Chapter 13)	Sell a naked put (Chapter 17)
Neutral bias	Buy a calendar spread (Chapter 14)	Write a covered call (Chapter 18)
	Buy a long straddle (Chapter 15)	Enter a butterfly spread (Chapter 19)

Trading Strategy Matrix

The trading strategies to be discussed in the following chapters are categorized based on two key variables: whether the trade benefits from neutral or directional price action, and whether the strategy is best initiated when implied volatility is high or low.

To use Table 11.1, first you must decide if you are bullish, bearish, or neutral on a given security. Next, assess the current level of implied volatility for the security in question. Finally, look at Table 11.1 to determine which strategies make the most sense, given your answers.

To show how you could use this table, consider the following scenario. Based on some technical analysis, you expect a given stock to rise in price. Since you are definitely bullish on the stock you will want to employ a directional trading strategy. Your next step is to assess the current relative volatility rank for that stock to determine if volatility is currently high or low. If you find that the relative volatility is at the low end of the spectrum, you see in the trading strategy matrix that the best choices in the "directional bias, low volatility" box are to buy a naked call or put or to buy a backspread. Assuming that your bullish assessment proves to be correct, these are the two strategies you should consider to maximize your profitability.

Overview of Trading Strategy Chapters

Chapter 12, Buy a Naked Option
Chapter 13, Buy a Backspread
Chapter 14, Buy a Calendar Spread
Chapter 15, Buy a Straddle
Chapter 16, Sell a Vertical Spread
Chapter 17, Sell a Naked Put
Chapter 18, Write a Covered Call
Chapter 19, Enter a Butterfly Spread

Chapters 12 through 19 discuss in detail one of the trading strategies that appears in the trading strategy matrix presented in

Table 11.1. Each trading strategy chapter contains a discussion of the strategy's primary purpose and the key factors involved in making the strategy work on a regular basis. Each chapter also includes an example trade. For each example trade you will find one or more of the following features:

- *Graph of underlying price action.* A bar chart depicting the type of market action to look for when considering a given strategy is included to help you visualize the type of situation in which a given strategy should be used (Figure 11.1).
- *Graph of option volatility.* A graph of the implied option volatility for the highlighted security is included to help you visualize whether volatility should be high or low for you to consider using a given trading strategy (Figure 11.2).
- *Option price grid.* A grid of option prices for the underlying security is included, with the option or options used in the example trade highlighted, to help you visualize the proximity to the at-the-money option and the expiration month(s) relative to the nearest expiration month (Table 11.2).
- *Risk curve graph.* Each chapter includes a graph displaying the risk curves for the example trade to help you visualize what the underlying security must do for the example trade

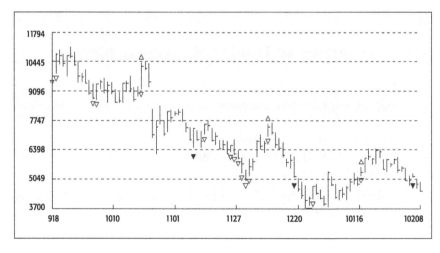

Figure 11.1   A buy puts signal for JDS Uniphase on February 6.

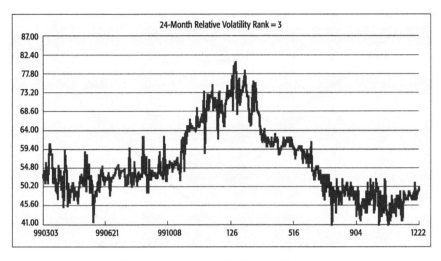

Figure 11.2   Toys "R" Us Implied Volatility.

Table 11.2   America Online Option Price Grid

		Puts			
		FEB **25**	**MAR** **54**	**APR** **89**	**JUL** **180**
47.5	Delta	−16	−22	−25	−27
	Bid	1.15	1.95	2.75	4.10.
	Asked	1.30	2.15	3.00	4.40
	Imp. V.	67.75	59.21	57.34	53.09
50	Delta	−27	−30	−32	−32
	Bid	1.65	2.50	3.30	4.90
	Asked	1.80	2.75	3.60	5.20
	Imp. V.	62.02	55.65	53.06	51.00
55	Delta	−52	−48	−46	−42
	Bid	3.60	4.70	5.60	7.00
	Asked	3.90	5.00	5.90	7.30
	Imp. V.	57.15	53.68	51.70	48.24
60	Delta	−74	−65	−59	−52
	Bid	6.90	7.80	8.50	9.90
	Asked	7.20	8.10	8.80	10.20
	Imp. V.	54.61	52.13	49.58	47.61
65	Delta	−88	−79	−71	−61
	Bid	11.20	11.60	12.10	13.30
	Asked	11.60	12.00	12.50	13.70
	Imp. V.	57.16	51.06	48.91	47.74

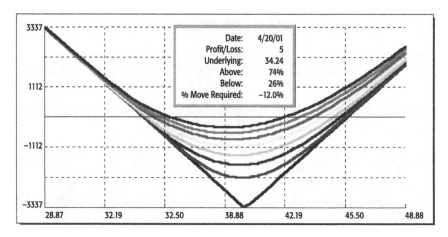

Date:	4/20/01
Profit/Loss:	5
Underlying:	34.24
Above:	74%
Below:	26%
% Move Required:	-12.0%

Figure 11.3   Reader's Digest buy straddle risk curves.

to make money. It also helps you visualize the worst-case scenario for the trade in question (Figure 11.3).

• *Position-management considerations.* Getting into a trade is often the easy part. It can be more difficult to decide under what circumstances you should exit the trade. Each strategy chapter contains a discussion of the most important position-management considerations for the selected trading strategy in general, and the example trade specifically.

As discussed in each strategy chapter, the key elements involved in using any strategy successfully are

• When to consider using the strategy
• When to enter a trade using the strategy
• When to exit with a profit
• When to exit with a loss

• *Profit-taking and loss-cutting guidelines.* Specific guidelines are set for each example trade for determining when to exit the trade. Specific rules are set for exiting with a profit and exiting with a loss. The trade exit criteria presented in each chapter are not intended to serve as hard-and-fast rules but as guidelines to help you understand the importance and potential benefits of planning for the various contingencies associated with each strategy.

- *The end result of the example trade.* Each example is carried through to exit to help you see how the position-management criteria set forth when the trade was entered eventually caused the trade to be exited.

NOTE

The guidelines set forth in the following strategy chapters are not presented as the only way to use a given trading strategy. In reality there is no single best way to trade options. However, instead of attempting to enumerate the different ways in which a given strategy might be used, the goal here is to show you one specific method executed from start to finish.

Over the years it has been observed that traders who follow a structured, disciplined approach to trading generally have a great deal more success than traders who make it up as they go along or who follow one set of rules one time and a different set the next time. A set of specific trading rules does not always generate the maximum profit from a given trade or series of trades. However, objective trading rules can keep a trader from making the major mistakes that tend to doom traders who rely on gut feelings.

Whether you use the guidelines set forth in each strategy chapter or develop your own set of guidelines is not important. What matters is that you gain an understanding of the importance of setting objective entry and exit criteria on an ongoing basis. In the long run, doing so gives you your best opportunity to succeed.

Chapter 12

BUY A NAKED OPTION

PURPOSE: To maximize the profitability of a market-timing call.

Key Factors

1. You have some reason to believe the underlying will move in a particular direction.
2. Low option volatility is a plus.
3. Enough delta and time remain until expiration to minimize time decay.

The strategy of buying a naked option is strictly a play on market timing. If your timing is good, you have the opportunity to leverage your gains by buying a call or put option rather than simply buying or selling short the underlying security. In fact, the only reason to consider buying a naked call or put option is that you expect a significant price movement by the underlying security within a specific time frame. Please note, however, that although market timing is a key element in implementing this strategy, it is not the *only* important factor.

The primary mistakes traders make when buying calls and puts are

- Relying solely on market timing to trade options
- Always buying out-of-the-money options hoping for the big score
- Buying options when implied volatility is high
- Buying options with little time left until expiration

Poor timing, time decay, and a decline in implied option volatility are the greatest enemies of option buyers.

Poor timing will undo a naked long call or put position every time. If you buy a call option and the underlying security declines significantly in price and does not rebound, you will invariably suffer a loss. The same will happen if you buy a put option and the price of the underlying security advances sharply and does not pull back. Therefore, it is imperative that you buy naked calls and puts only when you have a solid reason for believing that the underlying security is going to move in a particular direction.

Time decay can eat away a large portion of the option premium you pay if the underlying security fails to make the expected move within a relatively short period. If you buy an option whose price contains a great deal of time premium and volatility subsequently declines, the time premium built into the price of your option will decline, thus requiring an even greater move by the underlying to compensate. If your market timing is right, you may occasionally be able to get away with buying high-priced (i.e., high-volatility) options. However, if you buy out-of-the-money options often enough when volatility is high, the odds will invariably catch up with you.

In the long run it is critical to minimize the potentially negative effects of time decay.

To put the odds in your favor when buying naked options, use the following rules:

- Buy naked options only when you expect a significant price movement.
- Purchase options with a delta of 50 or more (for calls) and a delta of –50 or less (for puts).
- The lower the implied volatility, the better. Lower volatility means less time premium. However, this does not mean that you should never buy options if volatility is high. Rather, the higher the implied volatility, the further in the money and the shorter term the option you buy should be. This minimizes the amount of time premium you pay and reduces your exposure to time decay and a sharp decline in volatility.
- Buy options with at least 30 days (and preferably more) until expiration.

Following these rules will greatly improve your odds of success in the long run.

Two key elements to look for when selecting buy-naked-option trades are

1. Some catalyst to make you believe that a large price move is imminent
2. A way to take advantage of the expected move without being hurt by time decay or a decline in volatility after the trade is entered

Market timing is discussed in Chapter 8. For no other strategy is timing more important than when buying a naked call or put. The specific timing method used may vary from trader to trader.

Regardless of which timing method you use, there is no reason ever to buy a naked call or put option if you do not have some objective grounds for believing that the underlying security is about to make a significant move in price. Also, buying naked options when implied volatility is low increases your probability of profit by allowing you to buy cheap options.

Buying naked options when volatility is low gives you greater upside potential, as well as the opportunity to profit should option volatility increase in the near future because higher implied volatility translates into higher option prices. If volatility is high, you must take steps to minimize the amount of time premium you pay.

One use of options is to pick tops and bottoms while limiting your risk to a predetermined amount. Because of the limited-risk aspect of buying options, you can make a bet on a market top or bottom and simultaneously limit your risk to the amount you pay for the option if your timing turns out to be wrong.

Near the far right of the graph in Figure 12.1 is a solid down arrow on February 6, which indicates that a mechanical trading system has generated a signal to buy puts on JDS Uniphase (symbol: JDSU). In Figure 12.2, you can see that option volatility for JDSU options is neither extremely high nor extremely low. Nevertheless, with a relative volatility rank of 6, we know that the options are not cheap and that if we buy puts and volatility falls sharply, the price of the option could be adversely affected. Table 12.1 shows that the choices are to buy a March option with 39 days until expiration, a June option with 130 days, or a September option with 221 days. The February options will suffer the most from time decay since they expire the soonest.

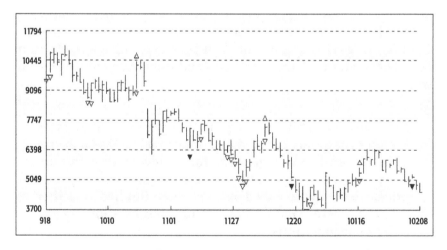

Figure 12.1   A buy puts signal for JDS Uniphase on February 6.

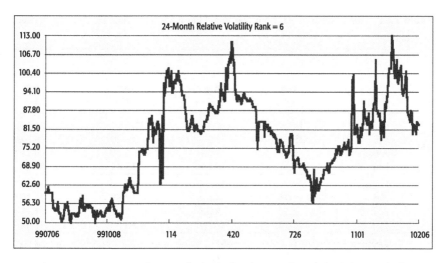

Figure 12.2   JDS Uniphase implied volatility (not exorbitantly high, but not low).

However, the time premium in the longer-dated options could collapse if volatility levels fall. With the relative volatility rank at 6, there is definitely room for volatility to fall. A sharp decline in volatility would cause the June and September options to lose a great deal of time premium. This combination of factors suggests that buying an in-the-money March option and selling it ahead of the last two weeks before option expiration is the best play. This limits the amount of time premium paid up front and thus limits the amount by which time decay can hurt this position.

With current option volatility in the middle of its historical range, Figure 12.2 shows a current relative volatility rank of 6. If we buy options here, we hope that volatility will rise, thus inflating the price of the option. However, we must also recognize that a sharp drop in volatility is a possibility.

Table 12.1 shows that the March 65 put has a delta of –72. This means that this option will move 0.72 points for every one point move in the underlying stock. This value also indicates that there is approximately a 72% probability that this option will be in the money—and thus retain some intrinsic value—at the time of March expiration. Most importantly, this option has

Table 12.1   JDS Uniphase Puts: Priority Is to Minimize Effects of Time Decay and a Decline in Volatility

		Puts			
		FEB **10**	**MAR** **39**	**JUN** **130**	**SEP** **221**
45	Delta	−16	−25	−28	−27
	Bid	−75	2.62	6.12	8.62
	Asked	1.00	3.00	6.50	9.00
	Imp. V.	100.51	90.16	85.38	85.83
50	Delta	−37	−38	−36	−33
	Bid	2.25	4.62	8.50	11.25
	Asked	2.50	5.00	8.88	11.75
	Imp. V.	96.18	87.75	83.87	85.54
55	Delta	−61	−51	−43	−38
	Bid	4.75	7.25	11.12	13.75
	Asked	5.12	7.75	11.62	14.50
	Imp. V.	89.12	85.79	81.95	83.05
60	Delta	−79	−63	−50	−44
	Bid	8.50	10.50	14.25	17.00
	Asked	9.00	11.00	14.75	17.50
	Imp. V.	86.41	83.05	80.88	82.29
65	Delta	−90	−72	−56	−49
	Bid	13.00	14.38	17.50	20.12
	Asked	13.75	14.88	18.25	21.12
	Imp. V.	92.23	82.15	79.44	81.76
70	Delta	−96	−80	−62	−53
	Bid	18.00	18.75	21.38	23.75
	Asked	18.50	19.25	22.12	24.50
	Imp. V.	NA	84.08	80.04	80.80

only 1.69 points of time premium built into it. For a put option this amount is calculated as follows:

$$\text{Current stock price} - (\text{strike price minus option price}) \text{ OR}$$
$$51.81 - (65 - 14.88) =$$
$$51.81 - 50.12 = 1.69$$

Many traders are reluctant to buy high-priced, deep-in-the-money options (this is not surprising because deep-in-the-money options cost more and offer less leverage). However, even if volatility falls sharply, only a small part of this option price will be affected because this option has only 1.69 points of time premium built into its price to begin with. Because volatility has room to fall, buying this particular option allows us to insulate ourselves from the potentially negative effect of a decline in volatility. In other words, no matter how far volatility levels might fall, this option can lose no more than 1.69 points as a result of that decline.

Figure 12.3 depicts risk curves for four dates leading up to March 2, which is two weeks before March option expiration. With JDS Uniphase trading at a price of 51.81, we purchased two March 65 put options at a price of 14.88 each (or $1487.50 per option). As a result, our total dollar risk for this trade is $2975. In other words, if we hold this option until expiration and JDSU is trading at 65 or above at that time, the March 65 put option will expire worthless and we will sustain a loss of $2975 dollars. This is our worst-case scenario for this trade.

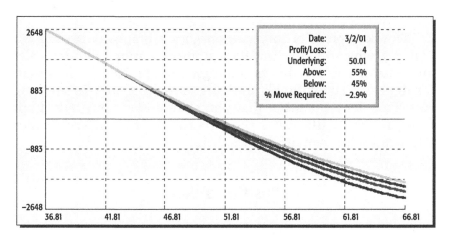

Figure 12.3   Buy 2 JDSU March 65 put options.

The graph in Figure 12.3 also depicts the negative effect of time decay. Note how the lines keep shifting lower and to the left with the passage of time. This has the effect of moving our break-even point further away as option expiration draws closer. To dampen the inevitable negative effects of time decay, we purchased a deep-in-the-money put option (a strike price of 65 with the underlying trading at 51.81) with a delta of −72.

If we were to hold this position until option expiration, our break-even price would be 50.12. A close below that price at the time of option expiration would result in a profitable trade. A close above that price at the time of option expiration would result in a losing trade, assuming we are still holding the option at that time. When this trade is entered the probability of JDSU being at or below our break-even price of 50.12 at the time of option expiration is 44%. If the stock falls below 50.12, we will enjoy point-for-point profit. In other words, for each point that the stock declines, the put option will gain one point.

Because you pay time premium on top of any intrinsic value to purchase an option, whenever you buy a naked call or put you have less than a 50% probability of making money if you hold the trade until expiration.

This key piece of information goes a long way toward explaining why so many traders lose money simply buying calls and puts. If you are always trading with a probability less than 50:50, it can be extremely difficult to make money in the long run. This does not mean that you should never buy naked options, it simply illustrates the importance of considering other strategies when conditions warrant.

Position Taken

Buy 2 March 65 puts at 14.88.

Maximum risk	−$2975
Delta	−72 × 2
Days to expiration	39

Probability of profit   44%
Current underlying price   51.81
Break-even price at expiration   50.12

The maximum risk on this trade is $2975. In the worst-case scenario (i.e., if the stock price goes up rather than down), we could simply hold this trade until expiration and lose no more than that amount no matter how far JDSU may rise. If we are not willing to risk the full $2975, we must devise a plan for cutting our loss. Also, in case JDSU falls in price, we need to devise a plan for determining when to take our profits.

There are no magic formulas for determining when to cut a loss. What is important is planning in advance to deal with your worst-case scenario.

Planning how to deal with the worst case is your only safeguard against emotional decision making, which can lead to devastating losses.

Here are two workable approaches in this case:

1. Choose some arbitrary dollar amount and place a stop-loss order at the appropriate price.
2. Figure 12.1 shows that JDSU recently hit a price of 64 and then fell sharply. We can use this price as a resistance point and decide that if the stock rallies above this point, our bearish outlook is wrong and we should exit the trade. While this is not an exact science, the rationale is easy to understand. The reason that we got into the trade in the first place is because we expect the stock to trend lower. If it rallies instead and takes out a key resistance price, our basis for entering the trade is no longer valid and we should exit.

For our purposes, we chose to hold the trade as long as JDSU stays below 64. Looking at the risk curves in Figure 12.3 we see that if JDSU rallied to 64 prior to March 2, we would lose between $1600 and $2100, depending on how soon the rally takes place. The loss becomes a little greater with each passing week due to time decay.

For taking a profit, it is wise to employ a staggered technique. This simply means that we will take some profits at the first good opportunity and then attempt to let our profits run on the remaining position.

- If an oscillator becomes oversold, we will sell one put to lock in a partial profit.
- We will look to exit the position entirely on or very soon after March 2. After that date we will want to exit the trade completely or roll out to another month. The reason for this is that the March options expire on March 16, and we would prefer to avoid holding a March option during the two weeks before expiration. As discussed in Chapter 5, time decay accelerates rapidly during the final two weeks before expiration.

There is no way to guarantee that this approach will maximize our profits or minimize our losses. Nevertheless, by having a predetermined plan for exiting the trade, we can avoid the emotional pitfalls that cause so many traders to freeze at exactly the wrong time.

Position Management

Stop-loss:

- Sell 2 March 65 puts if JDSU exceeds 64.
- Exit this trade after March 2.

Profit-taking:

- Sell 1 March 65 put if oscillator becomes oversold.
- Exit this trade after March 2.

As you can see on the graph in Figure 12.4, this trade could not have worked out much better. After only three days in the trade JDSU fell to 42.62 and became oversold. We were able to lock in a partial profit of $750 by selling one March 65 put at a price of 22.38.

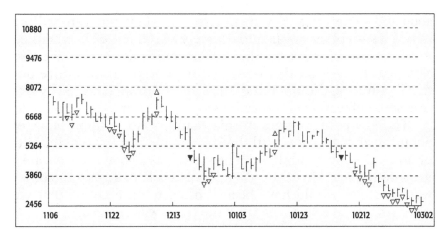

Figure 12.4 JDSU Price Falls, Generating a Profit for March 65 Puts.

After a brief one-day rally four days later, the stock then plummeted to 26.40 by March 2, allowing us to sell the second March 65 put at a price of 38.25, for a profit of $2338. In sum, this trade garnered a profit of $3088 on an initial investment of $2975, or a return of 104% (Table 12.2). Before you get stars in your eyes, you should realize that only a small percentage of trades work out as well as this one did. The purpose here is not to say, "Wow, look at this great trade!" but to illustrate the critical steps involved in trade selection and planning.

It should be noted that the return on this trade could have been much higher if we had bought lower-priced out-of-the-money options instead of the deep-in-the-money 65 puts. However, hindsight is always 20/20. At the time of the original signal our goal was not to throw caution to the wind and reach for the maximum profit. What we sought was a reasonable tradeoff between reward and risk.

This trade was entered into on the basis of a mechanical trading system. As with most systems, sometimes the signals are

Table 12.2 JDSU March 65 Puts

Long/Short	Quantity	Type	Price In	Last Price	$ + /–
Long	1	March 65 put	14.88	22.38	+$750
Long	1	March 65 put	14.88	38.25	+$2338

good and sometimes they are not. In a nutshell, we were willing to risk a sum of money (approximately $2100 if JDSU had rallied to 64) on a speculative bet that JDSU would fall in price. We also assessed the risk on this trade and took steps to minimize our risk by limiting the amount of time premium we paid and by setting some objective and specific stop-loss criteria.

The key point to note in this example is the importance of planning ahead to deal with both favorable and unfavorable situations. On one hand this can be viewed as a good trade because it made money. However, even if this trade had gone the other way, the loss would have been limited to an amount that we were willing to risk at the time the trade was entered.

Trade Result

Sold 1 March 65 put at 22.38.
Sold 1 March 65 put at 38.25.

Profit = $3088

KEY POINTS

If you feel compelled to pick a top or bottom, options—by virtue of their limited risk—can give you a great deal more staying power than would trading the underlying security. Nevertheless, if the reason you picked a top or bottom in the first place is no longer valid, you may consider cutting your loss and moving on rather than hoping that things will turn around.

The Great Paradox of Option Buying

Lesson A
The way to maximize your profitability on any single trade is to buy a far out-of-the-money option.

Lesson B
The way to maximize your profitability in the long run is to avoid Lesson A.

Chapter 13

BUY A BACKSPREAD

PURPOSE: As an alternative to buying naked calls or puts, buying a backspread affords the opportunity to profit from a market-timing call with some protection if wrong. It is also a good way to take advantage of low volatility.

Key Factors

1. You are expecting a particular market movement but want some protection if you are wrong.
2. There is low implied volatility (you hope volatility will rise after the trade is entered).
3. The ability to enter at a credit or a favorable volatility skew is a plus.

The strategy of buying a backspread involves writing an at-the-money or in-the-money call or put option and simultaneously buying a greater number of out-of-the-money options. (The ratio of options bought to options written can be 2:1, 3:2, 5:3, 11:10, or any other combination. The main point is that you buy more options than you write.) Ideally this trade is entered at a credit (i.e., you take in more money for the options you sell than you pay out for the options you buy), which offers you complete protection if your expected scenario turns out to be exactly wrong.

The backspread strategy can be used in a number of situations. Under the right circumstances this strategy is ideal for times when you feel compelled to pick a top or bottom but are concerned about the risk if you are wrong. It can also be used as an alternative to buying a naked call or put option if you expect a particular underlying price movement but are concerned that the move may not take place soon enough to keep a naked call or put option from experiencing serious time decay. There are two situations that generally offer the best opportunities for using backspreads.

1. *Situation A.* One use of this strategy is to enter a backspread when a given stock or futures market is experiencing a steep decline (or a sharp rally) that you think could reverse sharply at any time. If you buy a naked call option in this situation and the decline continues, you may very quickly find yourself with a large loss and thus in need of a major rally simply to get back to breakeven. In this situation, buying a backspread can give you a great deal more staying power than buying a naked option because it offers you some protection on the downside.

For example, say a stock you are following is plummeting and you believe that it is extremely oversold and due for a sharp rally. You might sell an at-the-money call option for 5.00 points and buy 2 one-strike, out-of-the-money options for 2.00 points each, or 4.00 points total. The end result is that you receive a net credit of 1.00 point ($100). Because you are long more calls than you are short, you have unlimited upside potential if you are correct and the stock rallies. If you are dead wrong and the stock continues to dive, you still stand to make $100 by virtue of taking in more premium than you paid out.

2. *Situation B.* You expect a particular stock or futures market to stage a substantial rally (or decline) but are concerned that it may take a while to play out. One benefit of a backspread (barring a sharp decline in option volatility) is that if it is properly constructed, it can give you very little dollar risk for a relatively long period. Thus, you retain the potential for unlimited profit, you have downside protection if the underlying security goes in exactly the opposite direction of what you expect, and you may

have little dollar risk for a lengthy period, even if the underlying fails to make a substantial move in either direction.

Whatever the situation, it often pays to use longer-dated options when trading a backspread. This gives you more time for a move to play out. Additionally, longer-dated options react more to changes in volatility. Thus, if you enter a backspread when volatility is very low, you have the potential to achieve windfall profits if volatility subsequently rises.

As with all option strategies, there is no free lunch. If the underlying security remains relatively unchanged or implied volatility declines sharply, this trade can generate losses.

The majority of the risk associated with a backspread occurs if this trade is held until expiration.

That is why it is recommended that backspreads not be held until expiration if the underlying security is trading within a price range that could result in substantial loss at expiration. For example, let's assume that based on the formation in the bar chart in Figure 13.1, we believe that Toys "R" Us has made a

Figure 13.1 Toys "R" Us daily price.

bottom and will soon stage a rally. This part of the analysis is based on whatever timing technique an individual trader decides to use and thus will vary from trader to trader. In this case we are trading based on a chart pattern involving a double bottom and a key reversal day.

One alternative would be to buy a naked call option. That would give us unlimited profit potential if Toys "R" Us does rally, with limited downside risk. However, let's say we are also concerned that this recent bottom will not hold and that the recent advance is just a rally in a bear market. Given these concerns, an alternative would be to write the the June 12.5 call and to buy a higher strike price (the June 17.5) in a ratio that results in receiving a credit by virtue of taking in more premium for the option we write than we pay out for the options we buy. In this example, a trade can be entered at a slight credit by writing 5 of the 12.5 calls and buying 11 of the 17.5 calls, as shown in Table 13.1.

The ideal circumstance for using a backspread is when you can write an option that is trading at a significantly higher im-

Table 13.1　Toys "R" Us Option Prices

		Calls			
		JAN 27	FEB 55	MAR 84	JUN 175
12.5	Delta	95	90	87	83
	Bid	3.25	3.37	3.50	4.00
	Asked	3.50	3.62	3.75	4.37
	Imp. V.	70.27	56.24	51.18	51.88
15	Delta	65	64	63	64
	Bid	1.25	1.56	1.87	2.43
	Asked	1.44	1.75	2.06	2.68
	Imp. V.	56.02	51.49	51.49	47.79
17.5	Delta	24	33	37	44
	Bid	.25	.56	.81	1.43
	Asked	.38	.75	1.00	1.62
	Imp. V.	52.36	52.15	50.38	47.83
20	Delta	5	13	18	28
	Bid	.00	.06	.31	.75
	Asked	.06	.18	.43	1.00
	Imp. V.	53.04	44.25	49.70	47.72

plied volatility than the option you buy. This gives you your greatest potential edge. At a minimum, you should look for an opportunity to write an option trading at a higher implied volatility than the option you plan to buy. The preceding example meets this minimum criteria (the 12.5 call is trading at an implied volatility of 51.88, and the 17.5 call is trading at an implied volatility of 47.83).

In sum, the backspread strategy can give a trader

- The courage to pick a top or bottom in the face of a strongly trending market
- The time to allow a market-timing call to work out without buying a naked call or put option
- The potential to profit from a significant increase in volatility

The trade shown in Figure 13.2 is entered on December 22 using June options. We will hold this trade for up to three months and hope for a large price movement and an increase in volatility. Option volatility for Toys "R" Us is currently at the low end of its historic range. It is certainly possible that volatility could fall

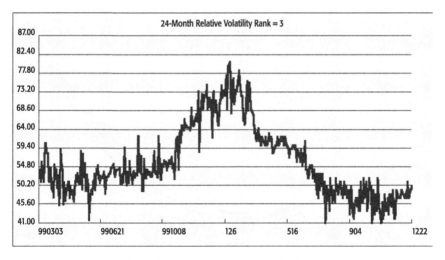

Figure 13.2   Toys "R" US implied volatility.

back within the 40 to 50 range and stay there for an extended period. Nevertheless, there is clearly room for volatility to rise if the
stock starts to move. As we will illustrate, a rise in volatility can
have an extremely beneficial effect on a backspread.

The graph in Figure 13.3 shows risk curves for three dates—
January 20, February 20, and March 20. With Toys "R" Us trading at 15.69, we purchased 11 June 17.5 call options each at a
price of 1.62 and simultaneously wrote 5 June 12.5 call options
at a price of 4.00.

This trade nets an initial credit of $212, which represents the
maximum profit potential if we were to hold this trade until
June expiration and Toys "R" Us was trading below 12.5. If Toys
"R" Us rallies sharply, we have unlimited profit potential by
virtue of being long more call options than we are short. In contrast, if Toys "R" Us resumes its recent downtrend and declines
sharply, we still stand to profit by virtue of having received the
initial $212 credit when we entered the trade. In reality we will
not likely collect this amount since we are only planning to hold
the trade for a maximum of three months.

If this trade is held for three months—barring any changes in
implied volatility—our break-even points are 10.04 on the downside and 19.30 on the upside.

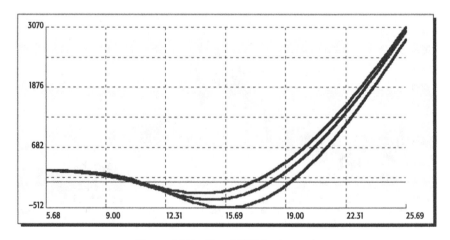

Figure 13.3   Toys "R" Us backspread.

Each risk curve drawn on the graph in Figure 13.3 shows the potential profit or loss as of a given date based on the price of Toys "R" Us (the current price of 15.69 is in the middle, with plus or minus 10-point increments on either side). A close examination reveals that the dollar risk increases with each line (i.e., as time decay begins to work against us) if the stock stays in a narrow range. The maximum risk on this trade of $2266 would be experienced only if we held this position until expiration and Toys "R" Us closed at exactly 17.5. This graph illustrates the one negative to using the backspread strategy: If the market makes a decent move up or down, that's fine. The primary risk associated with this trade is that Toys "R" Us might simply drift within a narrow range.

Position Taken

Sell 5 June 12.5 calls at 4.00.
Buy 11 June 17.5 calls at 1.62.

Credit obtained	$212
Current underlying price	15.69
Days to expiration	175
Break-even price at expiration	Below 10.40 or above 19.30

Before following this trade through until exit, let's examine a few other factors affecting backspreads in general.

Backspreads versus Naked Calls and Puts

Backspreads are generally used in place of buying a naked call or put option. Option trading involves many tradeoffs, and backspreads are no exception. If you use a backspread instead of buying a naked call option, you gain certain advantages but you also give up something to gain these advantages.

The primary difference between these two positions is what happens if the stock goes down. Figure 13.4 depicts the risk

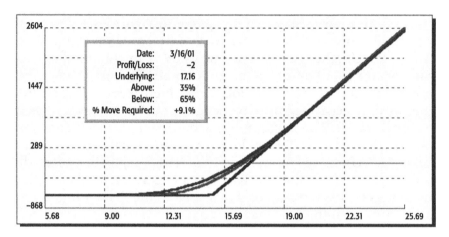

Figure 13.4   Toys "R" Us buy 3 March 15 calls at 2.06.

curves for a trader buying 3 March 15 calls at 2.06. At any price below 17.06 this trade will show a loss and at any price below 15 it will lose 100%. Conversely, the backspread shown in Figure 13.5 will lose *less* money as the stock falls and could eventually earn a profit if the stock falls far enough.

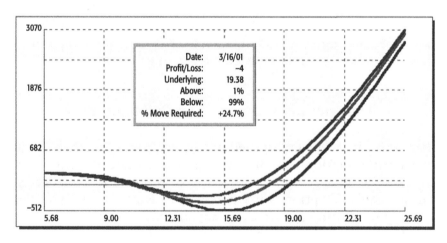

Figure 13.5   Toys "R" Us backspread risk curves.

Volatility and Backspreads

The advantage to entering a backspread when volatility is low is that you can gain additional profit if volatility rises after you enter the trade. This trade was entered on December 22. Figure 13.6 shows the expected return as of March 16 if volatility is unchanged from its level when the trade was entered. Figure 13.7 depicts the expected returns based on three volatility levels as of March 16. The lowest curve represents expected return if volatility falls to 40, the middle curve represents a volatility of 60, and the uppermost curve represents volatility rising to 80 three months from now. To fully appreciate the impact of volatility, let's assume that the stock is trading at 19 on March 16. At a volatility of 40, the trade would show a loss of $490. At a volatility of 60 the trade would show a profit of $180. At a volatility of 80 this trade would show an open profit of $795. The upside potential created by a rise in volatility is the reason you should ideally enter backspreads when volatility is low. Also, remember this can work against you in reverse. If you enter a backspread when volatility is very high and volatility subsequently collapses, the expected return on your trade will likely plummet also.

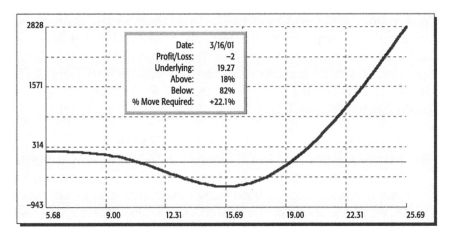

Figure 13.6   Toys "R" Us backspread risk curvess (3 months later if volatility is unchanged).

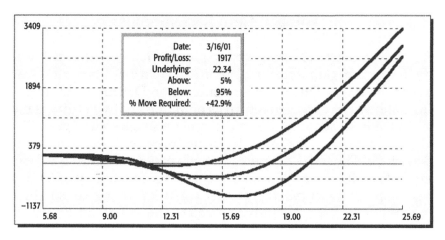

Figure 13.7   Toys "R" Us backspread (3 months later if volatility is at 80, 60, or 40).

Managing a backspread position can be extremely subjective. First, you have unlimited profit potential on one side and a defined profit potential on the other side. Also, you must be concerned about time decay, particularly, the longer the trade goes on with the underlying drifting in a narrow range. The other concern is the prospect of getting assigned on the option you write. If the underlying moves far enough in the expected direction, the option you wrote will eventually trade deep in the money. As the amount of time premium narrows, the likelihood of exercise and assignment becomes greater. For purposes of setting objective position-management rules for this trade, we will first look at what we know for sure about this trade. The two things we know for sure are that

1. Our profit potential on the downside is $212.
2. Our maximum risk is $2268 and can occur only if we hold this trade until expiration. The effect of time decay can be seen in Figure 13.8, which shows risk curves as of February 15, April 15, and June 15 (option expiration). Notice how risk increases significantly at expiration.

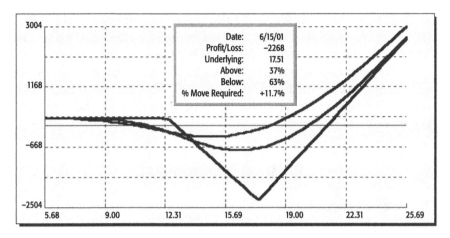

Date:	6/15/01
Profit/Loss:	−2268
Underlying:	17.51
Above:	37%
Below:	63%
% Move Required:	+11.7%

Figure 13.8   Toys "R" Us as of 2/15, 4/15, and 6/15 (expiration).

Our first step is simply to decide that we will not hold this trade until expiration. This relieves any worry about experiencing the maximum potential loss. The good news regarding this trade is that unless volatility plunges to new lows, there is almost no way to lose a lot of money for at least the next three months because volatility is already low and there is a great deal of time left until expiration. We will hold this trade for a maximum of three months.

Looking at the historical volatility for Toys "R" Us, we calculate that a two-standard-deviation move for Toys "R" Us over a 90-day period would be 5.64 points. In other words, if Toys "R" Us falls to 10.04 or rises to 21.33 at any time during the next three months, this would constitute a statistically significant move for this stock. As a result, we decide to close the trade if either of these price levels is pierced. Looking again at the risk curves in Figure 13.4, we can see that if the stock fell to 10.04 the trade would be about at break-even, and the stock would then have to rally significantly to achieve a meaningful profit. We are hoping that the Toys "R" Us price will rally. If, however, the stock collapses later on and we have the opportunity to get out at about break-even, we will take the opportunity to do so. Notice in Figure 13.4 that if we had bought naked calls and the stock collapsed, we would be faced with a large percentage loss.

If the stock rallies to 21.33 within the next three months, we can anticipate a profit of $700 to $1700, depending on how soon the rally takes place and the level of volatility at the time our target price is reached.

Position Management

Trade exit criteria:

- If Toy "R" Us rallies to 21.33 or falls to 10.04, exit the entire trade.
- If neither target is hit within three months, exit the entire trade.

As you can see in Figure 13.9, Toys "R" Us shot higher in early January, closing on January 4 above our upside target of 21.33. This trade could have been closed out on January 4 for a quick profit of $1443 (see Table 13.2). Obviously, not every trade will work out this well or this quickly.

Nevertheless, this example illustrates two key factors in option trading success:

1. The importance of recognizing each trade's weak spot
2. Planning in advance to deal with the worst-case scenario

In this example, we felt that Toys "R" Us had bottomed out, but we were not highly confident that the recent low would hold. This is why we used the backspread strategy rather than

Table 13.2 Toys "R" Us Backspread

Long/Short	Quantity	Type	Price In	Last Price	$ + /−
Short	5	June 12.5 calls	4.00	10.75	−$3375
Long	11	June 17.5 calls	1.62	6.00	+$4818

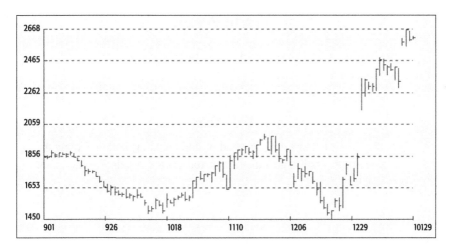

Figure 13.9 Toys "R" Us rallies to upper price target.

simply buying a naked call. We also recognized that the worst case would occur if Toys "R" Us drifted in a narrow range. To limit our dollar risk under such circumstances, we bought options with six months left until expiration and planned to exit them after only three months.

The purpose of this example is not to show you how easy it is to make money trading options. The purpose is to emphasize the benefits of intelligent position management. Too many traders put on a trade like this and simply wait to see what happens. This is usually a mistake. It will be very beneficial to your long-term results if you always have a plan when you enter any trade. This includes setting criteria for deciding when to take a loss. It is no fun to lose money in trading, but the fact remains that cutting a loss and moving on is very often the proper move to make. It is much easier to implement this important step if you have planned in advance to cut your loss based on some reasonable criteria rather than to react by making an emotional decision to an adverse price movement after the fact.

If you already know when you enter a trade what has to happen for you to exit, the number of mistakes you make in trading will decline significantly.

Trade Result

Upside target of 21.33 exceeded on January 4.
Profit = $1443

KEY POINT

Do not plan on holding a backspread position until expiration. Exiting the trade before expiration guarantees that you cannot sustain the maximum potential loss.

Chapter 14

BUY A CALENDAR SPREAD

PURPOSE: To take advantage of differences in option volatilities.

Key Factors

1. The option sold should be trading at a volatility at least 15% higher than that of the option bought.
2. Do not use this strategy if option volatility is high (the lower the volatility, the better).
3. No more than 45 days remain until the option sold expires.
4. You have some reason to believe the underlying will remain within a particular range of prices.

One area of opportunity unique to option trading is that each option for a given underlying security generally trades at a different implied volatility level. Sometimes the disparity between the volatility of different options can be quite large. This situation gives alert traders the opportunity to take advantage of disparities between the implied volatility levels of different options. The idea is simply to write an option that is trading at a significantly higher implied volatility than the option you buy.

One way to take advantage of a large disparity in volatility is to buy an option that is trading at a given implied volatility level and simultaneously write a different option that is trading at a much higher implied volatility. This gives you an edge because you are buying a cheaper option and selling a more expensive option. Whenever you trade a spread, you should look for an opportunity to write an option trading at a higher volatility than the option you buy. This type of opportunity is also discussed in Chapter 13, Buy a Backspread, and Chapter 16, Sell a Vertical Spread. Each of these strategies trade different options within the same expiration month. Another useful way to take advantage of volatility disparities is by trading a calendar spread.

A *calendar spread* is entered into by buying one option of a given strike price and expiration month and simultaneously writing an option with the same strike price but a different expiration month that has less time until expiration than the option you bought. Buying a July 50 call option on a particular stock and simultaneously selling a June 50 call option is an example of a calendar spread.

As a rule of thumb, the time to enter a calendar spread is when a near-term option is trading at an implied volatility that is at least 15% above the implied volatility of the farther-out option of the same strike price.

A calendar spread is a neutral position. In other words, you benefit from having the underlying security remain within a particular range of prices and by allowing time decay to work in your favor. The width of this profitable range of underlying prices is determined by the difference in the implied volatility levels of the options used. Thus, the higher the implied volatility of the option sold relative to the implied volatility of the option bought, the higher the probability of profit.

A calendar spread is a limited-risk position, but there are two dangers in trading a calendar spread. First, if the underlying security advances or declines significantly, this trade can become very unprofitable. Second, a major decline in option volatility can put you in a position in which you have little or no chance of making money (more on this topic later).

The less time left until expiration for the options you sell, the better (assuming you receive enough premium to make the trade worth taking in the first place). In addition, by trading options with deltas between 35 and 65 for calls and from –35 to –65 for puts, you can establish a range of underlying prices above and below the current price that can yield a profitable trade. Outside of these delta values you can get into a situation in which the underlying security must make a fairly substantial move in price to generate a profit, which can greatly reduce your probability of profit. The exception to this rule is that you can trade a strike price that is within one strike price of the underlying security price, regardless of the deltas of the options involved.

To maximize your potential when trading calendar spreads:

- Enter a calendar spread only when the option you sell is trading at an implied volatility at least 15% above the implied volatility of the option you purchase.
- Trade calendar spreads only when the relative volatility rank is below 6 (on a scale of 1 to 10). The ideal situation is to trade a security with a relative volatility rank of 1 or 2 that also meets the other criteria. The reason for this suggested criterion is simply that if volatility increases after you enter a calendar spread, you stand to reap windfall profits because the price of the longer-term option you bought will rise much more than the short-term option you wrote.
- Sell options with no more than 45 days (and preferably fewer) remaining until expiration.
- Trade options with delta values between 35 and 65 (calls) or from –35 to –65 (puts), or trade options that are no more than one strike price away from the current underlying price.

Make certain that the overall level of option volatilities for the underlying security is relatively low before entering a calendar spread. This is extremely important because a sharp decline in volatility has the potential to wipe out any chance you have of making money when trading a calendar spread. Remember, you are paying more for the option you buy than you are receiving for the option you write. In terms of its effect on option prices, a decline in volatility lowers all boats. Therefore, if volatility falls dramatically, you have more to lose from a decline in the price of the option you bought than you do to gain from a decline in the price of the option you sold. As a result, in order to put the odds as far in your favor as possible you should focus your search for calendar spreads on stocks or futures markets with low relative volatility rankings.

In Table 14.1 and Figure 14.1 you see an ideal setup for a calendar spread using options on America Online (AOL).

- The near-term at-the-money put option (the February 50 put) is trading at an implied volatility level (62.02%) that is 17% higher than the implied volatility (53.06%) for the same option two months out (the April 50 put).
- The overall level of option volatility for AOL is extremely low (a relative volatility rank of 1).

Table 14.1   America Online Volatility Skew

		Puts			
		FEB 25	**MAR** 54	**APR** 89	**JUL** 180
47.5	Delta	−16	−22	−25	−27
	Bid	1.15		2.75	4.10
	Asked	1.30		3.00	4.40
	Imp. V.	67.75		57.34	53.09
50	Delta	−27	−30	−32	−32
	Bid	1.65	2.50	3.30	4.90
	Asked	1.80	2.75	3.60	5.20
	Imp. V.	62.02	55.65	53.06	51.00
55	Delta	−52	−48	−46	−42
	Bid	3.60	4.70	5.60	7.00
	Asked	3.90	5.00	5.90	7.30
	Imp. V.	57.15	53.68	51.70	48.24
60	Delta	−74	−65	−59	−52
	Bid	6.90	7.80	8.50	9.90
	Asked	7.20	8.10	8.80	10.20
	Imp. V.	54.61	52.13	49.58	47.61
65	Delta	−88	−79	−71	−61
	Bid	11.20	11.60	12.10	13.30
	Asked	11.60	12.00	12.50	13.70
	Imp. V.	57.16	51.06	48.91	47.74

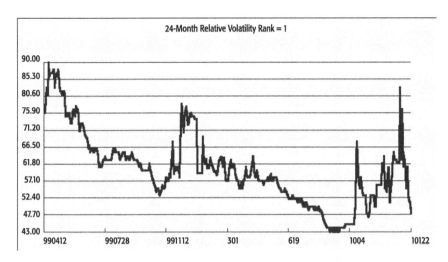

Figure 14.1 America Online implied volatility.

- There are only 25 days left until the February option expires. This means that the effect of time decay will begin to work in our favor quickly, which is ideal when writing options.
- The deltas for these options (–32 and –27) are outside the preferred –35 to –65 range, but the options are within one strike price of the underlying price, so this trade still qualifies as a neutral trade.

One other favorable factor to look for when considering a calendar spread is an underlying security in a trading range. For an example of a trading range market, look at the graph of AOL in Figure 14.2. In this graph you can see that AOL stock traded in a range of 31 to 62 for almost 4 months. In a properly constructed calendar spread, you will generally not be at risk to lose a lot of money unless the underlying security makes a significant price movement. Focusing on securities with easily identifiable support and resistance levels above and below the current price gives you a better chance of making money with calendar spreads. Underlying securities with established support and resistance levels are ideal candidates for calendar spreads because the underlying security is required to stage a breakout to a new (at least short-term) high or low for the trade to turn into a loss

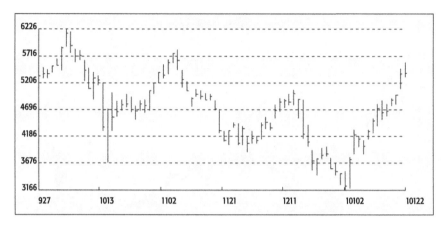

Figure 14.2   America Online in a trading range.

of any meaningful size. Nevertheless, although support and resistance levels are important, the difference between the volatility of the option you buy and the option you write remains the key element in selecting calendar spreads to trade. A trading range is simply another favorable factor to look for.

As shown in Figure 14.3, using this strategy establishes a position that will generate a profit only if the underlying security stays within a particular range of prices. If the underlying secu-

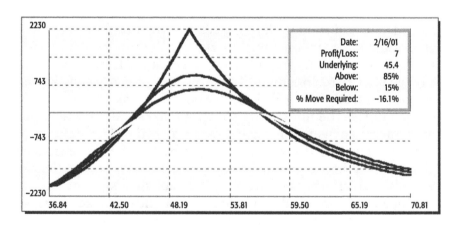

Figure 14.3   America Online calendar spread risk curves.

rity moves outside this range, losses will occur. The width of this profit range is determined by the size of the difference in the implied volatility of the option bought versus that of the option sold. This underscores the importance of having as wide a spread as possible between the volatility levels of the option bought versus the option sold.

NOTE

Before trading a calendar spread on a futures contract, you should make certain that both the options you are going to use trade based on the same underlying futures contract month. For example, January, February, and March T-bond options trade based on the March T-bond futures. April, May, and June options trade based on the June futures contract. You should not trade one option based on the June futures and another option based on the March futures because futures contracts of different months can trade independently of one another. This is especially true in the grain markets (e.g., Corn, Soybeans, Wheat) and the soft markets (e.g., Coffee, Sugar). If you trade options based on different futures months, you run the risk of losing money on both options if the underlying futures contracts move in opposite directions. For example, it is not uncommon for July Soybeans to rally while November Soybeans decline. If you were long a November call option and short a July call option, you could end up losing money on both sides of the trade. Do not make the mistake of putting yourself in this potentially dangerous situation.

The graph in Figure 14.3 displays risk curves for three dates leading up to option expiration. With AOL trading at 53.81, we bought 10 April 50 puts at 3.60 and sold 10 February 50 puts at 1.65. The cost of this position is $1995. Our maximum profit potential is approximately $2230. The amount of profit potential is only an approximation because although we can state with certainty how much the February option will be worth at the time of February expiration at a given underlying price, we can only estimate the price at which the April option will be trading at that time. This is because the volatility of that option may rise or fall in the meantime, thus inflating or deflating the price of our long option accordingly.

Of key importance in viewing these risk curves (or the risk curve for any calendar spread) is to note the break-even points. As you can see in Figure 14.3 (assuming no change in implied volatility levels), this trade will a show a profit at February option expiration if the price of AOL is between 45.34 and 56.64. Based on the historic volatility of AOL stock when this trade was entered, there is a 43% probability that the price of AOL will be within this price range at the time of option expiration.

As always, there is no way to know in advance how this trade will work out. All we can do is put the odds as much in our favor as possible. To that end, with this example trade we

- Chose a market with low option volatility (a relative volatility rank of 1)
- Sold a call option with an implied volatility 17% higher than the volatility of the option we bought
- Sold a call option with less than 45 days until expiration (25 days in this case)

In this trade we exceeded our target delta range (of –35 to –65 when trading puts), but the strike price (50) is within one strike price of the current stock price (53.81)

The biggest risk we assume when entering this trade is that AOL will trade outside the profit range of 45.34 to 56.64. The key question to answer when setting position management criteria is how to deal with this possibility. Our choices are as follows:

- Establish some arbitrary stop-loss level.
- Simply hold the trade until near expiration and hope that the stock is within our profit range.
- Establish some alternate exit criteria.

In this case we decided to hold the trade until expiration unless one of the following two criteria is met:

1. If the time premium on the February 50 put declines to 0.125 or less, we will exit the entire trade. If the stock falls and the short February 50 put trades deep in the money, we will close

the trade to avoid being exercised on the short puts. If the stock rises and the amount of time premium built into the price of the February 50 put falls to 0.125, we can either close out the entire trade or buy back the February puts and continue to hold the long April puts in hopes that AOL stock will fall. This would be a subjective decision, however, and would expose us to greater risk.

2. If the trade shows an open loss in excess of $1000, we will exit the trade. Inspecting the risk curves, we find that in order for this loss level to be reached the stock price would have to fall below 42 or rise above 62.50. Based on the historic volatility for AOL, the probability of this happening is only about 26%.

Position Taken

Buy 10 April 50 puts at 3.60.
Sell 10 February 50 puts at 1.65.

Approximate maximum profit	$2230
Approximate maximum risk	–$1994
Approximate probability of profit	43%
Current underlying price	53.81
Break-even price at expiration	Above 45.34 *and* below 56.64

Position Management

Stop-loss:

- If the time premium on the February 50 put declines to 0.125, exit the entire trade.
- If the trade shows an open loss greater than $1000, exit the entire trade.

Profit-taking: As long as trade shows a profit, hold as close to expiration as possible.

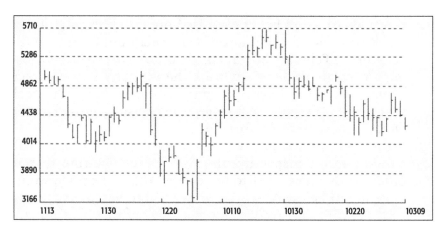

Figure 14.4 America Online stays in profitable range.

As you can see in Figure 14.4, AOL stock rallied for a couple of days after this trade was entered and then fell back below 50. Fortunately, it did not fall far enough to cause our short option to trade deep in the money, so we were able to let the trade ride. At the close of the day before February expiration, the April put could be sold at a price of 4.00, generating a profit of $400 on a 10-lot. The February 50 put could be bought back at a price of 0.75, generating a profit of $900 on a 10-lot. As a result, this trade netted a profit of $1300 (Table 14.2).

Trade Result

Table 14.2 AOL Calendar Spread Result

Long/Short	Quantity	Type	Price In	Last Price	$ + /–
Long	10	April 50 Puts	3.60	4.00	+$400
Short	10	February 50 Puts	1.65	0.75	+$900

KEY POINT

The ideal time to enter a calendar spread is when the implied volatility of the option you sell is at least 15% higher than the implied volatility of the option you buy.

A Decline in Volatility Is Deadly to Calendar Spreads

To understand why low volatility is one of the suggested guide-lines in selecting calendar spreads, you must understand the impact that changes in volatility can have on this type of spread. In a calendar spread you are long an option that has more time left until expiration than the option you are short. As discussed in Chapter 6, the more time left until expiration, the more sensitive an option will be to changes in volatility. As a result, if volatility rises after you enter a calendar spread, you stand to gain a wind-fall profit because that increase in volatility will serve to inflate the price of the option you are long far more than it will the price of the option you have written. Conversely, if volatility falls dra-matically after you enter a calendar spread, you stand to take un-expected losses because this decline in volatility will serve to deflate the price of the option you are long far more than it will the price of the option you have written.

The graph in Figure 14.5 depicts three risk curves for the AOL calendar spread we just discussed. Each line represents the profit or loss we could expect from this trade as of February op-tion expiration, depending on the level of implied option volatil-ity at that time.

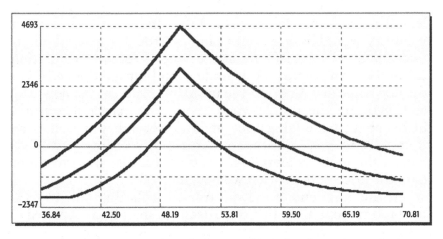

Figure 14.5   America Online calendar spread (volatility of 83%, 63%, or 43%).

If you look again at Figure 14.1, you will see that implied volatility for AOL options had recently ranged as low as 43% and as high as 83%. In Figure 14.5 you can see three risk curves. Each curve represents the expected profit or loss from our calendar spread example trade, with the only difference being the level of option volatility at the time of February option expiration.

- The upper curve depicts the profit or loss we could expect at the time of February expiration if volatility rose back up to its most recent high of 83%.
- The middle curve is based on a volatility of 63%.
- The lowest curve assumes that option volatility fell back to its recent low of 43%.

Please take a moment to study these curves because they dramatically illustrate why volatility is so important when trading calendar spreads.

Remember, at expiration the February call that we wrote will have no time premium left, only intrinsic value. However, the price of the April call option that we bought will be highly dependent on the level of volatility at that time. If volatility rises to high levels, the price of our long option will be inflated accordingly. If volatility falls to lower levels, the price of our long option will be deflated accordingly.

It would be optimistic to assume that volatility will rise back to its recent high of 83% after this trade was entered. Nevertheless, it is important to understand the effect that such a rise in volatility would have on our example trade. If the April 50 put traded at a volatility of 83% at the time of February expiration, the break-even points on this trade would expand from 45.34 on the downside and 56.64 on the upside to 39.61 on the downside and 68.06 on the upside. As a result, the expected return is higher at any underlying price, and the probability of profit soars from 43% to 88%. Clearly an increase in volatility greatly enhances the profit potential of this trade because it serves to inflate the price of the option we bought.

At the other end of the spectrum, if volatility falls to 43%, the profit potential for this trade declines sharply (as depicted by the lowest risk curve in Figure 14.5). In addition, the range of underlying prices that will generate a profit contracts significantly. Accordingly, as volatility declines, our probability of profit is dramatically reduced.

In this example, if implied volatility fell from the current level of 53% to 43%, AOL stock would have to be trading between 47.25 and 53.50 at the time of February option expiration for this calendar spread to show a profit. This is an extremely narrow range of profitability. A close at any price outside of this range would result in a loss.

The purpose of this example is to illustrate the importance of entering calendar spreads when implied volatility levels are relatively low. If you enter a trade when implied volatility is low, there is no guarantee that volatility will then rise or that it will not fall to even lower levels. Nevertheless, if you enter a calendar spread when the relative volatility rank for the underlying security is high (6 to 10), you put yourself in a very dangerous situation. As the risk curves in Figure 14.5 clearly illustrate, a sharp decline in volatility can leave you with almost no chance of making a meaningful profit when trading a calendar spread!

Chapter 15

BUY A STRADDLE

PURPOSE: To take advantage of low volatility or quiet market conditions to profit from the next big price move.

Key Factors

1. You have some reason to expect a sizable price movement by the underlying.
2. Option volatility is low.
3. Adequate time remains until expiration.
4. There is an equal opportunity to make money whether the underlying rises or falls.

The strategy of buying a straddle involves buying a call option and a put option simultaneously. The options can be of the same strike price or different strike prices. Buying a call and a put with different strike prices is called a strangle. For our purposes we will use the terms *straddle* and *strangle* interchangeably.

On a strictly mathematical basis, buying a straddle probably has the lowest probability of generating a profit of any strategy covered in this book. Consider this: Whenever you buy a call or a put option, time decay can eat away a large portion of the option premium you pay, particularly if the underlying security fails to make the expected move within a relatively short period.

When you buy both a call and a put option, this negative effect is multiplied.

The only reason to ever consider buying a straddle is that you expect a significant price movement by the underlying security, but you are uncertain as to the direction of the next move.

Several other important factors should be considered before buying a straddle. If you enter a position without giving any consideration to these other factors, even a significant price movement by the underlying security may not be enough to generate a profit on the trade.

The key elements to consider when selecting buy-straddle trades are these:

- Some catalyst to make you believe that a large price move is imminent.
- Low implied option volatility (the lower the implied volatility, the less time premium you pay).
- Adequate time, that is, allowing enough time until option expiration for the underlying security to make a move big enough to generate a profit.

Most traders make the mistake of not giving the underlying security enough time to make a significant price move. Many traders would rather buy short-term options because they cost less than longer-term options (those with at least 60 days until expiration) and are in fact more sensitive to underlying price changes. Unfortunately, when it comes to buying a straddle, this can be a costly mistake in the long run.

Generally, when you buy a straddle, the underlying security must make a fairly significant move in one direction or the other in order to generate enough of a gain on the profitable option to offset the loss on the other option. If you buy a straddle using options with 30 days left until expiration, you are putting yourself in a situation in which the underlying security must make an immediate and substantial move for you to profit. Doing this on a regular basis puts you on the path to trading failure.

One useful rule of thumb in buying straddles is to buy options with a minimum of 74 days left until expiration. Why 74 days? By buying options with at least 74 days left until expiration, you know that you can hold the position for a full 60 days without getting into the last two weeks before expiration, when time decay really accelerates. You should generally exit any straddles before the last two weeks of trading prior to expiration unless one of the options you are holding is deep in the money and you feel strongly that the trend will continue in the direction of that option (up for a call, down for a put). In this case you may get more bang for your buck by holding the deep-in-the-money option a while longer. This is a subjective decision that must be made on a trade-by-trade basis.

When buying a straddle, you should make the trade as neutral as possible. In other words, since you are not choosing a direction, you want to have an equal chance of making money whether the underlying security price rises or falls. One way to facilitate this is to consider the deltas for the options you buy and try to make the trade as close to delta neutral as possible.

Whenever you buy a straddle, you are exposing yourself to time decay not only on one position but on two. As a result, it is extremely important that you do not buy straddles on stocks or futures markets when the implied volatility for the options on that security is relatively high. If you buy a straddle when option volatility is high,

- You pay more to buy the options than you would if volatility was low, thereby reducing your probability of profit.
- If option volatility subsequently collapses, you may have little hope of generating a profit. This is because the amount of time premium built into the price of your options will collapse also, thus requiring the underlying security to move even further to make up for this loss of time premium.

Conversely, buying options when implied volatility is low allows you to buy cheap options. As a result, your dollar goes further. Focusing on low-option-volatility situations also gives you the opportunity to profit should option volatility increase after you enter the trade. It is certainly possible that a stock or futures contract with high implied volatility may rally or decline enough to generate a profit on a long straddle. Be aware that just because implied volatility happens to be low does not necessarily mean that it will increase significantly any time soon, nor that it cannot go even lower.

The goal in option trading is to put the odds as far in your favor as possible each time you enter a trade. Paying a lot of time premium on both a call option and a put option is not consistent with this goal and should generally be avoided.

Ideally, you should buy a straddle when the relative volatility rank for the underlying security is 1, 2, or 3 (on a scale of 1 to 10). As you can see in the graph in Figure 15.1, the relative volatility rank for Reader's Digest is 1. This objective measure indicates that the options for this stock are currently cheap.

Additionally, there is no reason to ever buy a straddle if you do not have some objective reason to believe that the underlying security will soon make a significant price movement. As you can see in the daily bar chart in Figure 15.2, Reader's Digest

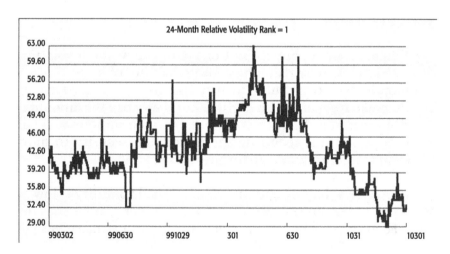

Figure 15.1   Reader's Digest implied volatility at a low level.

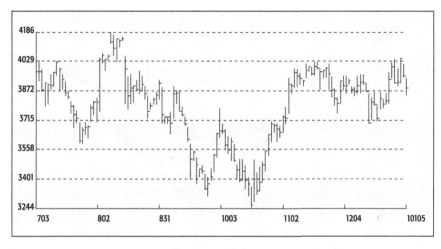

Figure 15.2   Reader's Digest daily price in a trading range.

stock has been trading in a fairly narrow 3-point range for three months. A further inspection of this bar chart reveals that Reader's Digest has a history of trading in a narrow range and then breaking out. Since Reader's Digest has already spent a considerable amount of time chopping back and forth within a trading range, it is not unreasonable to expect a meaningful breakout at some point soon.

This combination of factors—low option volatility and an extended trading range—suggest that the time may be right to buy a straddle on Reader's Digest.

With Reader's Digest trading at a price of 38.88, we purchase 6 April 40 calls at a price of 2.50 and 6 April 40 puts at a price of 3.12. The total dollar risk associated with this trade is equal to the amount of premium paid to buy the options, or $3375. The graph in Figure 15.3 depicts risk curves for six dates leading up to option expiration (also see Table 15.1).

The risk curve lines in the graph in Figure 15.3 clearly depict the negative effect of time decay that will result if Reader's Digest continues to trade in a narrow range. Notice how each line drops lower and spreads out wider as time decay eats away at the price of both options. If Reader's Digest fails to make a sustained

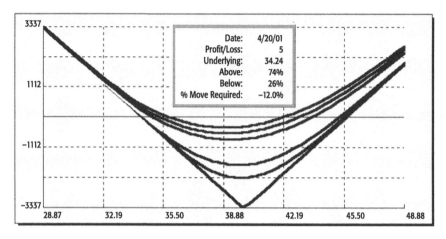

Figure 15.3 Reader's Digest Buy-Straddle Risk Curves.

price movement in one direction, either up or down, our loss becomes bigger and our break-even prices move out further as time goes by.

To give ourselves as much chance as possible of a profit on this trade,

- We bought options with 106 days (more than three full months) left until expiration. Giving the underlying security time to move is crucial to trading long straddles profitably.
- We made the trade delta neutral (our net delta is –6). This gives us an equal chance of making money whether the stock goes up or down.

If we were to hold this position until option expiration, our break-even prices are 34.24 on the downside and 45.72 on the upside. If we are still holding this position at expiration and Reader's Digest is not outside of that range, the trade will result in a loss. When the trade was entered, there was a 26% probability that Reader's Digest would be below 34.24 at expiration and a 21% probability that it would be above 45.72 at expiration. As a result, if we hold this trade until expiration, we have about a

Table 15.1 Reader's Digest Option Price Grid

		Calls				Puts			
		JAN 14	FEB 42	APR 106	JUL 197	JAN 14	FEB 42	APR 106	JUL 197
35	Delta	95	88	80	76	-4	-11	-19	-23
	Bid	3.88	4.37	5.12	6.12	-.06	.31	.94	1.62
	Asked	4.25	4.75	5.62	6.62	.31	.56	1.19	1.88
	Imp. V.	40.75	37.20	33.36	32.38	45.52	35.54	34.27	34.31
40	Delta	35	42	49	54	-64	-57	-50	-45
	Bid	.44	1.12	2.12	3.25	1.44	2.00	2.75	3.50
	Asked	.69	1.37	2.50	3.62	1.69	2.37	3.12	3.88
	Imp. V.	32.50	31.10	30.61	30.43	30.60	31.85	31.46	32.08
45	Delta	1	8	22	33	-98	-91	-77	-66
	Bid	.00	.00	.56	1.44	5.75	5.87	6.12	6.62
	Asked	.25	.25	.81	1.69	6.25	6.37	6.62	7.12
	Imp. V.	59.25	33.50	28.37	28.81	NA	16.12	31.62	32.47

1:4 chance of making money. Clearly, we stand to benefit from Reader's Digest making a move sooner rather than later.

As this example clearly illustrates, the primary risk involved with the "buy a straddle" strategy is that the underlying security must make a significant price move for this trade to break even, let alone to generate a profit.

Position Taken

Buy 6 April 40 calls at 2.50.
Buy 6 April 40 puts at 3.12.

Maximum risk	–$3375
Net delta	–6
Days to expiration	106
Probability of profit	27%
Current underlying price	38.88
Break-even price at expiration	Above 45.72 or below 34.24

The maximum risk on this trade is $3375. In the worst-case scenario (i.e., if Reader's Digest was trading exactly at $40 per share at the time of April option expiration), we can simply hold this trade until expiration and lose no more than that amount. If we are not willing to risk the entire $3375, we must devise a plan for cutting our loss. We also must have a plan for taking our profits if a major price movement does occur before option expiration.

There are no magic formulas for determining when to cut a loss. What is most important is planning in advance to deal with the worst case.

There are several choices:

- If you are willing to risk the entire amount used to enter the trade, you can simply hold the trade until just before expiration.

- You can plan to exit the trade ahead of the last two weeks before option expiration. In the risk curve in Figure 15.3, notice that time decay really accelerates during the final weeks before expiration. Buying options with a minimum of 74 days left until expiration is a good rule of thumb. You may consider exiting the trade if it has not generated a profit prior to the last two weeks before option expiration. By doing this you eliminate the possibility of sustaining a complete loss.
- Select a dollar amount that you are comfortable risking and exit the entire trade if that amount is reached or exceeded.

In this trade we are not comfortable risking the entire $3375. As a result, we decide to risk one-half of our maximum potential loss. If at any time this trade experiences an open loss of $1700 or more, we will exit the trade, cut our loss, and move on to the next trade.

For taking a profit, we can use one of several approaches. First, we can take some profits at the first good opportunity and then attempt to let our profits run on the remaining position. We can also establish a profit target for the trade as a whole. To accomplish these goals we established the following criteria:

- If one of the options doubles in price, we can sell three calls and three puts in order to lock in a partial profit.
- After that we can use a trailing stop of one-half of our peak open profit (every time our profit reaches a new high we will adjust our trailing stop upward) to lock in profits unless and until one of the options triples in price. At that point we would simply exit the entire trade, take our profit, and move on to the next trade.
- An alternative is to set a fixed profit target of, say, 20% on the entire position on a closing basis. In this case, we would exit this trade if we achieved an open profit of $675 or more on a closing basis. The advantage of this method is that you may often be presented with opportunities to take a profit. The downside to this alternative is that you never give yourself a chance for a really big winning trade.

There is no guarantee that this approach will maximize our profits or minimize our losses. Nevertheless, by having a predetermined plan for exiting our trade we can avoid the emotional pitfalls that cause so many traders to freeze at exactly the wrong time. We also avoid the "I make it up as I go along" syndrome that causes so many traders to fail in the long run.

Position Management

Stop-loss: Close trade if loss reaches –$1700 (half the maximum risk).

Profit-taking:

- Close the one-half position if either option doubles in price, and then use a trailing stop of one-half of the open profit on the remaining position(s).
- Alternatively, close the entire trade if a net profit of $675 is achieved.

As Table 15.2 shows, this trade worked out well, generating a profit of $1050 in just 14 trading days. In Figure 15.4 you can see that Reader's Digest advanced slightly for a few days before selling off to close at 32.68 on January 26.

There are any number of ways to manage a long straddle. We could have sold part of our position to lock in a profit and held the rest hoping for a big score. In this case, because we had established a profit target of $675 and had that target exceeded by almost $500 after only 14 trading days, it seemed like a good opportunity to take our profit and move on. This illustrates the potentially subjective nature of establishing position-management criteria. It also illustrates the advantage of having your trade-exit criteria in place when the trade is entered. Too many traders

Table 15.2   Reader's Digest Trade Result

Long/Short	Quantity	Type	Price In	Last Price	$ +/–
Long	6	April 40 calls	2.50	0.25	–$1350
Long	6	April 40 puts	3.12	7.12	+$2400

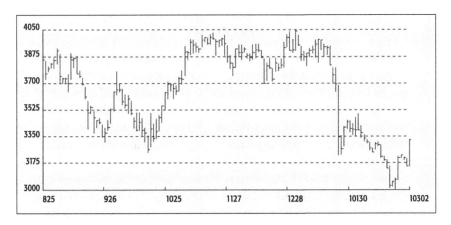

Figure 15.4 Reader's Digest daily prices.

make it up as they go along, taking an early profit one time, missing a huge move, and then vowing to ride the next trade only to see a quick profit vanish completely.

One of the biggest dangers involved in managing a long straddle position is overstaying your welcome. Often, profits are available for only a very short time. Many traders have a tendency to hold on, hoping for a huge price move, only to see their profits disappear when the market goes back into the original trading range.

What is important to note in this example is how setting objective exit criteria when you enter the trade allowed us to take a profit of $1050 dollars while risking $1700.

Trade Result

Stock close on January 26 at 32.68.
Twenty percent profit target exceeded; entire position exited.

Profit = $1050

KEY POINTS

When buying a straddle, focus on low-volatility situations and be certain to allow enough time for the underlying security to move before time decay begins to kick in. When exiting a straddle, consider taking profits on part of your position as soon as they are available. Then, if you wish, you can hold your remaining positions and hope for a big score. The alternative is to establish a reasonable profit target and exit completely if that target is reached.

Holding onto a straddle long enough to realize a profit can be very difficult psychologically. Many stock and futures traders learn early in their investment careers the importance of cutting a loss. However, being too quick to cut a loss after entering a long straddle is often a mistake. You must give this strategy time to work. Once you buy a straddle, this trade can show a loss for weeks or even months at a time. Then suddenly the underlying makes a big move, your profit objective is reached, and it is time to pull the trigger and exit the trade.

The reality is that along the way there is very little psychological gratification and you must be willing to stare at a reasonable loss day after day while waiting for the underlying to move. Too often traders get sick and tired of staring at a loss and decide to close the trade, often just before the underlying makes a move that could have made the trade profitable.

Chapter 16

SELL A VERTICAL SPREAD

PURPOSE: To put time decay and high volatility to work in your favor without the unlimited risk of writing naked options.

Key Factors

1. Implied volatility is higher than average (the higher, the better).
2. There is an identifiable support (or resistance) level.
3. You have the opportunity to sell an option as far out of the money as possible (delta 40 or less) while still receiving enough premium to make the trade worth taking.
4. Favorable volatility skew is a plus.

It is widely asserted that the majority of money made trading options is made by those who write options rather than by those who buy options. This is primarily a function of the fact that options are a wasting asset and that each option will always lose its entire time premium by the time it expires. Thus, any option that is out of the money at expiration will expire worthless. It is estimated that 60% or more of all options that are out of the money at the time they are written eventually expire worthless. This gives option writers an advantage. The big drawback they face is that writing naked options entails assuming unlimited risk in exchange for a limited profit potential.

Selling a vertical spread allows traders to write options without being exposed to the risk of unlimited loss. By selling an out-of-the-money call (or put) option and simultaneously purchasing a further-out-of-the-money call (or put) option, a trader can profit from time decay or a decline in volatility, or both, while defining his maximum risk. This strategy also allows traders to take advantage of extremely high option volatility or a particular market-timing opinion.

To maximize your potential when selling a vertical spread:

- Use this strategy only when implied option volatility is high (in order to maximize the amount of premium you receive for the option you write) or at least was recently very high and is now declining.
- Look for key levels of support (when selling puts) or resistance (when selling calls) for the underlying security, and then sell an option whose strike price is at or beyond that price level.
- Sell call options with a delta no greater than 40 and sell put options with a delta not less than −40 (the idea is to write out-of-the-money options that have a low probability of expiring in the money).
- Sell options with no more than 60 (and preferably fewer) days until expiration so as to maximize the beneficial effect of time decay.
- Whenever possible, look for situations in which you can sell an option trading at a higher implied volatility than the option you are buying.

If you believe that a stock or futures market is likely to rally, remain flat, or at least not decline very far, you may consider writing a vertical put spread. This is often referred to as a *bull put* spread. If you believe that a stock or futures market is likely to fall, remain flat, or at least not advance very far, you may consider writing a vertical call spread, or *bear call* spread.

The key to properly employing the "sell a vertical spread" strategy is finding situations in which the implied option volatility is high enough to allow you to receive enough premium to justify entering this trade with its limited profit potential.

Writing options when implied volatility is high allows you to write expensive options. This is a requirement when selling vertical spreads because it allows you to maximize the amount of premium you receive when entering the trade. Writing options when option volatility is high also gives you the opportunity to profit should option volatility decline in the near future.

Option writing can also be used in place of option buying to take advantage of a market-timing call if implied volatility is very high. Naïve traders often make the mistake of buying options when implied volatility is high. This stacks the deck against them by causing them to buy expensive options. The implication of buying expensive options is that the underlying security must move that much further to compensate for the additional time decay. A subsequent decline in volatility also serves to reduce the price of the option purchased. These factors can present huge obstacles for a trader to overcome.

If you believe that the underlying is likely to move strongly in a particular direction but implied volatility is high, you can sell a vertical spread on the other side of the market to profit if the expected price move occurs (by selling put spreads if you expect the underlying to rise or selling call spreads if you expect the underlying to fall). This is where you need to apply whatever market-timing method you prefer to indicate that a rise or fall in price is likely. This part of the analysis is based on whatever timing technique a trader decides to use.

There are several key factors to notice in Figures 16.1 and 16.2 and Table 16.1.

- In Figure 16.1 you can see that IBM is attempting to establish a support level at 80.06.

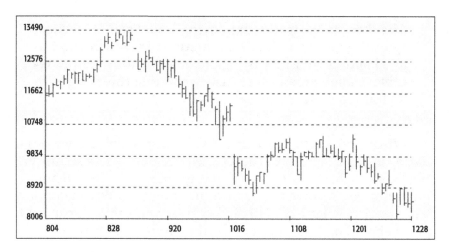

Figure 16.1   IBM – A support level forms at 80.06.

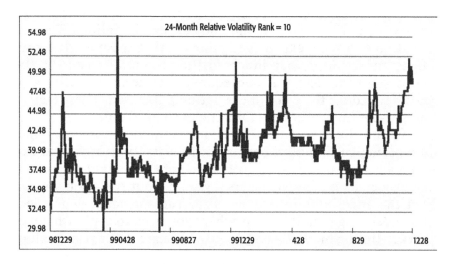

Figure 16.2   IBM Relative Volatility Rank is 10.

- In Figure 16.2 the relative volatility rank for IBM options is 10, the highest decile. This is an objective measure indicating that the options for this stock are currently expensive and that this may be a good time to write options on the stock.
- In Table 16.1 the option we are looking to write (the Febru-

Table 16.1   IBM Put Delta Not Less Than −40

		Puts			
		JAN 21	FEB 49	APR 113	JUL 204
70	Delta	−9	−14	−18	−20
	Bid	1.12	2.06	3.62	4.62
	Asked	1.50	2.31	3.87	5.12
	Imp. V.	83.91	67.38	57.77	50.59
75	Delta	−19	−22	−26	−26
	Bid	2.00	3.12	4.87	6.12
	Asked	2.25	3.37	5.37	6.75
	Imp. V.	77.83	63.65	55.61	49.34
80	Delta	−31	−33	−33	−33
	Bid	3.00	4.62	6.50	8.12
	Asked	3.38	5.12	7.12	8.75
	Imp. V.	69.69	61.61	53.45	48.70
85	Delta	−45	−43	−41	−39
	Bid	5.12	6.50	8.62	10.37
	Asked	5.75	7.12	9.25	11.00
	Imp. V.	69.81	58.18	51.79	47.84
90	Delta	−58	−54	−49	−45
	Bid	7.75	9.12	11.12	13.00
	Asked	8.38	9.75	11.75	13.62
	Imp. V.	66.08	56.22	50.13	47.27
95	Delta	−70	−64	−57	−51
	Bid	11.12	12.50	14.25	15.87
	Asked	11.75	13.12	14.87	16.50
	Imp. V.	63.15	56.27	49.84	46.59

ary 80 put) has 49 days left until expiration and a delta of −33. In other words, when we entered the trade there was a 67% probability that the option written would expire worthless. These are both within our guidelines (not more than 60 days until expiration and a delta of 40 or less for the option we write) for selling vertical spreads.

The graph in Figure 16.3 shows risk curves for five dates leading up to option expiration. With IBM trading at 85.25, we can sell 6 February 80 put options at a price of 4.62 ($462.50 per option) and simultaneously purchase 6 February 75 put options at

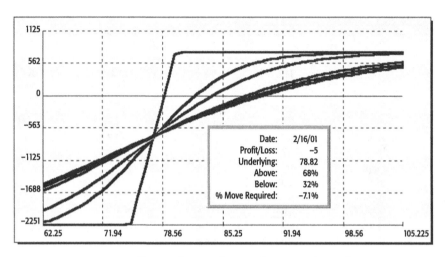

Figure 16.3   Risk curves for IBM short vertical spread.

a price of 3.37 ($337.50 per option). Our maximum profit potential is equal to the amount of the credit we receive when we enter the trade, which is $725 (1.25 points × $100 × 6 contracts). Our maximum risk of $1875 would occur if we were still holding this position at option expiration and IBM was then trading at 75 (i.e., the lower strike price) or lower.

Following the guidelines set out earlier for this strategy:

- We identified a market with high option volatility.
- We sold a put option with a delta between 0 and –40 (the February 80 put had a delta of –33).
- We sold a put option with less than 60 days until expiration (49 days in this case).
- We sold an option with a higher implied volatility than the option we bought.

Every option strategy offers some tradeoff. We can accurately state that there is a 68% probability that IBM will be above our break-even price of 78.82 at option expiration. As mentioned in Chapter 1, however, in order to properly assess our risk we must also look at what could happen to this position before expiration. As you can see, the danger of experiencing our maximum potential loss before expiration is low. However, one thing to consider when writing options is that profit potential is limited. In this example, our maximum profit potential is $725 while our maximum risk is 2.5 times as great ($1875). In this case, the good news is that we have a 68% probability of making money. The bad news is that we have a reward-to-risk ratio of only 1:2.5.

Based on these observations we recognize that if we were to let this trade experience the maximum potential loss, it would take three subsequent profitable trades just like it to offset the loss on this trade. Because our reward-to-risk ratio is 1:2.5, we must do whatever we can to make certain that this trade never reaches its maximum loss potential.

Position Taken

Sell 6 February 80 puts at 4.62.
Sell 6 February 75 puts at 3.37.

Maximum profit	$725
Maximum risk	–$1875
Probability of profit	68%
Current underlying price	85.25
Break-even price at expiration	78.82

Position management is very important for option trading success. Our biggest concern with this particular trade is that we have a maximum risk of $1875 but a maximum profit potential of only $725. As a result, our biggest priority in managing this trade is not to allow a large loss to occur that could take many subsequent trades from which to recover.

In this case we will establish our stop-loss criteria first. To reduce our risk-to-reward ratio from 1:2.5 to 1:1, we simply decide to exit this trade if it reaches an open loss of $725. If this occurs, we will exit the position, cut our loss, and move on. By so doing, only one such similarly profitable trade would be required to recoup our loss.

To determine when we might need to exit this trade to cut our loss, we first look at the risk curves and determine approximately how far the stock must move to generate a loss equal to our maximum profit potential. By examining the risk curve for January 5 (one week after the trade is entered), we find that the trade would generate a loss of approximately $725 if IBM fell to 77.50 by January 5. We then look at the bar chart for the underlying security itself. What we want to see is some easily identifiable and meaningful support level above this price (for a call, or below this price if we are selling puts). In other words, for our trade to be stopped out, the underlying security must take out a meaningful support or resistance level rather than just experiencing a random pullback in price.

Looking again at the bar chart for IBM in Figure 16.1, we see a support level at 80.06. So this trade fulfills the requirement just discussed. In other words, for our stop-loss level of 77.50 to be reached, IBM must first take out the support level at 80.06. In the meantime, as long as this support level holds, our trade will start to show a profit. For taking a profit we will use a simple technique. We will take our profit if we reach 80% of the maximum profit potential for this trade. The maximum profit potential is $725, so if we have an open profit of $580 or more, we will simply take our money and run. This can happen in one of three ways:

1. A rise in the price of IBM stock
2. A sharp decline in volatility
3. The passage of time

If one or more of these factors combine to give us 80% of our profit potential, we will take our profit and move on at that point rather than holding out for the last dollar and giving IBM the chance to fall back and jeopardize our profit. In summary, IBM must decline below 77.50 for our stop-loss to be triggered. Any type of market action other than an immediate price decline leaves us with a high probability of making money on this trade.

To give yourself the best chance of success in trading credit spreads:

• Look at a risk curve as of option expiration to determine your maximum profit potential.
• Look at risk curves before option expiration to see how far the underlying must go against you to trigger a loss equal to

(or at most up to 20% more than) your maximum profit potential.

- Look at a daily bar chart. Ideally there should be a major support level (if selling puts, or a major resistance level if selling calls) between the current price of the underlying and the hypothetical stop-loss point identified in Step 2).

The bottom line is this: You don't want to risk much more than your maximum profit potential on the trade. In addition, you want to see a situation in which the underlying must first take out a major support or resistance level before it can reach your stop-loss point.

Position Management

Stop-loss:

- Close trade if loss reaches –$725 (maximum profit times 1).
- Alternatively, we could close the trade if IBM drops below 80.06, taking out the latest level of support.

Profit-taking: Close trade if profit reaches $580 (80% of maximum profit).

As we had hoped, IBM rallied after the trade was entered, thus resulting in declining put option prices. As you can see in Figure 16.4, within three weeks IBM rallied sharply and our initial profit target of $580 was exceeded on January 18. Table 16.2 shows the net result of this trade.

This example illustrates an important point when writing options: You generally should not hold out for the last dollar.

To understand this concept, consider the change in the reward-to-risk ratio since the trade was first entered. We had already achieved $600 of our maximum $725 profit potential. As a result, we had only another $125 of profit potential remaining. Thus, our reward-to-risk ratio had shifted from $725 potential reward versus $1825 potential risk to $125 potential reward

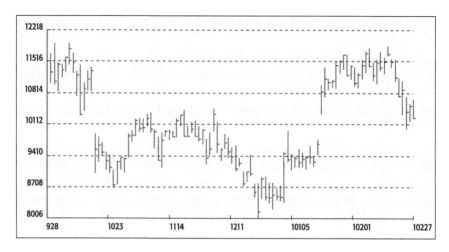

Figure 16.4   IBM rallies, profit taken on January 18.

Table 16.2   IBM Bull Put Spread Result

Long/Short	Quantity	Type	Price In	Last Price	$ + /–
Short	6	February 80 puts	4.62	0.50	+$2475
Long	6	February 75 puts	3.37	0.25	–$1875

versus $2375 potential risk. In other words, if we continued to hold this trade, we would be risking $2375 to make another $125. At this point the potential reward no longer justifies assuming the potential risk.

Trade Result

Profit target was reached on January 18.
Profit = $600

KEY POINT

When writing options, do not hold out for the last dollar.

Chapter 17

SELL A NAKED PUT

PURPOSE: To use high option volatility to accumulate stock below current market prices.

Key Factors

1. Extremely high implied volatility exists (the higher, the better).
2. There is an identifiable support level.
3. You want to own the underlying security.

Selling a naked put is a highly specialized strategy that most traders will never use and that quite frankly, many traders never should use. It involves nothing more than writing a naked put option on a given underlying security. Once this trade is entered, one of three outcomes will occur:

1. The stock will remain above the strike price of the put option and the option will expire worthless. In this case the writer of the option keeps the entire premium he or she originally collected when the option was written.
2. The price of the stock will fall below the strike price of the option written, the option will be exercised, and the writer of the option will be assigned (i.e., required to purchase 100 shares of stock at the strike price).
3. The writer of the put option will buy back the option before outcome 1 or 2 occurs.

This strategy is used primarily by sophisticated investors who are interested in accumulating shares of stock in a particular company but who for one reason or another are not willing to commit to buying the shares at the moment. It is best suited for *value investors*, who typically accumulate a position of meaningful size in a stock after the stock declines in price and are willing to hold the position for a reasonably long period. It is ill suited to short-term traders or *momentum investors*, who generally attempt to buy high and sell higher.

The most important consideration when selling a naked put is whether you want to own the stock. If the answer is no, or if you are not really sure, you should not use this strategy. To understand why, let's consider the primary benefit of this strategy as well as the worst-case scenario. Investors who use this strategy generally do so in an effort to acquire stock at a price below the current market price. Here is how that happens.

Say a stock is trading at a price of $85 per share. At the same time the 80 strike price put option is trading at a price of $3. You could buy the stock at $85 per share or you could write a put option with a strike price of 80 and collect a premium of 3 points (or $300). If you buy 100 shares of stock at $85 per share and it declines to $77 per share, you will lose $800. If you had written a put option at a strike price of 80 for 3 points and the stock declines to $77 per share, you would be at break-even. In other words, if the stock is put to you, your effective buy price is $77 per share (equal to the strike price minus the premium collected, or 80 minus 3). This is the benefit of writing naked puts. The disadvantages are these:

- If the stock rallies sharply, you will not participate in that rally beyond the option premium you collected.
- If the stock falls sharply, you still have significant downside risk.

To maximize your potential when selling a naked put:

- Use this strategy only after you have analyzed the prospects for the underlying company and have consciously decided that you are definitely willing to buy the stock.

- Use this strategy only when implied option volatility is high (to maximize the amount of premium you receive for the option you write).
- Look for a key level of support for the underlying security and then sell an option whose strike price is close to or below that price level.
- Sell put options with a delta between 0 and –50 (in other words, write out-of-the-money options to put time decay to your advantage).
- Sell options with no more than 60 days (and preferably fewer) until expiration (also to maximize the beneficial effect of time decay).

The key to employing the "sell a naked put" strategy correctly is to find a stock that you are willing to buy and whose options are presently trading at extremely high volatility levels.

In Figure 17.1 you can see that after a rally, IBM has pulled back toward its recent support level of 80.06. Figure 17.2 shows

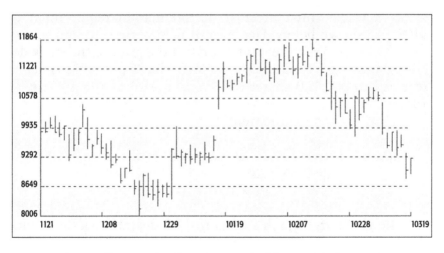

Figure 17.1   IBM – A support level forms at 80.06.

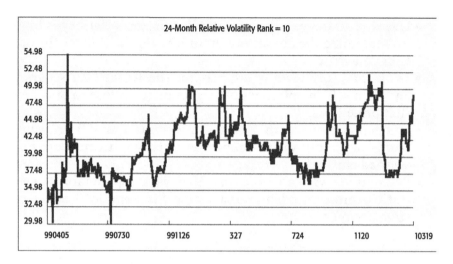

Figure 17.2　IBM volatility rank is a 10.

that implied volatility for IBM options is extremely high. For an investor who is willing to buy IBM stock, this represents a good setup for writing a naked put option. In Table 17.1, you can see that the April 85 put can be written for a premium of 3.60 points, or $360 per contract.

To write one IBM April 85 put with IBM stock trading at 92.56, a trader must meet an initial margin requirement of $1095, as shown below. However, it is important to understand that this margin requirement can rise if the price of the stock declines, and that ultimately the writer of the 85 put option may be required to buy 100 shares of IBM at a price of $85 a share, or $8500.

Initial margin requirement:

$$(((\text{Stock price} \times 20\%) - (\text{stock price} - \text{strike price})) \times 100)$$
$$(((92.56 \times .20) - (92.56 - 85)) \times 100)$$
$$((18.51 - 7.56) \times 100) = 10.95, \text{ or } \$1095$$

The risk curve graph in Figure 17.3 depicts risk curves for three dates leading up to option expiration. With IBM trading at 92.56, we sold 1 April 85 put at a price of 3.60 ($360). Our

Table 17.1 IBM Put Delta Not Less Than −50

		Puts			
		APR **32**	**MAY** **60**	**JUL** **123**	**OCT** **214**
70	Delta	−4	−7	−12	−14
	Bid	1.10	1.70	3.00	4.00
	Asked	1.35	1.95	3.30	4.40
	Imp. V.	83.04	69.73	60.84	53.50
75	Delta	−9	−12	−17	−19
	Bid	1.60	2.45	4.00	5.20
	Asked	1.85	2.75	4.30	5.60
	Imp. V.	76.44	66.19	58.16	51.74
80	Delta	−17	−20	−24	−24
	Bid	2.40	3.40	5.30	6.60
	Asked	2.70	3.70	5.70	7.10
	Imp. V.	71.52	62.02	56.29	50.18
85	Delta	−27	−29	−30	−30
	Bid	3.60	4.70	6.80	8.40
	Asked	3.90	5.00	7.30	8.90
	Imp. V.	67.20	58.45	54.00	49.13
90	Delta	−39	−39	−38	−36
	Bid	5.30	6.60	8.60	10.50
	Asked	5.70	7.00	9.10	11.00
	Imp. V.	64.09	56.93	51.54	48.20

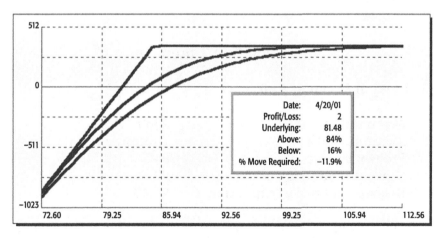

Figure 17.3 Risk curves for IBM short put.

maximum profit potential is equal to the amount of the credit we receive when we enter the trade, which is $360. If we hold this option until April expiration, one of two things will happen:

1. The option will expire out of the money and we will keep the $360 premium.
2. The option will expire in the money and we will buy 100 shares of IBM stock at $85 a share.

Following the guidelines set out earlier for this strategy:

1. We identified a stock in which we wish to accumulate a position (IBM).
2. We waited until the option volatility for that stock was extremely high (relative volatility rank of "10").
3. We sold a put option with a delta between 0 and –50 (the April 85 put had a delta of –27).
4. We sold a put option with less than 60 days until expiration (32 days in this case).

Looking only at the risk curve at expiration we can accurately state that there is an 84% probability that IBM will be above our break-even price of 81.40 at option expiration.

Position Taken

Sell 1 April 85 put at 3.60.

Maximum profit	$360
Maximum risk	Unlimited
Probability of profit	84%
Current underlying price	92.56
Break-even price at expiration	81.40

Our initial position-management criteria for this trade are fairly straightforward. We will either collect the premium if the stock stays above the option's strike price or buy the stock if it falls below the strike price.

Two different worst-case scenarios are associated with selling a naked put. The first occurs if the stock goes way up; the second occurs if the stock goes way down.

If the stock rallies, the good news is that we stand to make the equivalent of 3.60 points by virtue of having written a put option. If the stock advances more than that, we will gain no additional profit. For example, if the stock rallies 10 points, we might end up wishing that we had simply bought the stock. However, by writing a naked put we made a conscious decision to try to buy the stock at a lower price, and for now we must be satisfied to collect the option premium for the put we wrote. If we want, we can always write another put and start the same process again.

If the stock falls, the good news is that we will have the opportunity to buy it at a lower price than if we had bought the stock rather than writing the put option. The danger is that the stock will fall significantly below the strike price of the put option we wrote. Should this occur and the stock be put to us, we may quickly be saddled with a large open loss on our stock position. When a stock is trading at 92.56, having the opportunity to buy it a price of 81.40 sounds very enticing. However, if the underlying company comes out with a surprisingly bad earnings announcement and the stock gaps down 30 points overnight, the prospect of buying the stock at 81.40 no longer sounds like such a great proposition. Unfortunately, if you are short a naked put, you will have no choice but to either buy back the put—most likely at a significant loss—or buy the stock at the strike price and hope that it does not decline much more before rising back into profitable territory. The prospect of facing this very situation is why this strategy is best suited for investors who are already comfortable accumulating and holding a position in a stock for a reasonable length of time. It also illustrates the need for thorough investigation of the prospects for the underlying company before writing a naked put.

In this example we have decided that we are willing to buy IBM stock if it is put to us. Therefore, our position-management rules are fairly simple: We will hold the option until expiration and either collect $360 in premium or buy the stock at an effective price of 81.40. In light of the worst-case scenario on the downside, we must also establish some criteria for exiting the stock position if it continues to decline.

One Method for Managing Stock Position If Assigned

There are any number of ways to manage a stock position once entered. However, our specific concern in this case is deciding what we will do if the stock is put to us and its price continues to decline. One method worth considering is to risk the amount you saved. For example, in this trade we could have bought IBM stock outright at a price of 92.56 per share. Instead, we wrote the 85 put and collected 3.60 points of premium. As a result our effective purchase price if the stock is put to us is 81.40 (85 − 3.60). If the stock had stopped declining at that price, we would have saved ourselves 11.16 per share compared to buying the stock outright when it was at 92.56. Some traders might simply earmark this stock position as a long-term holding. Others might look at recent support levels and attempt to identity a good place to stop themselves out if the stock continues to decline. One other alternative is to use the amount that you saved by initially writing the naked put as a stop-loss value. Let's see how that would work in this example.

If the stock declines and we buy it at an effective price of 81.40, saving 11.16 per share, we can then place a stop-loss order to sell the stock if it falls to 70.24. This value is arrived at by subtracting the amount we saved by writing the option initially (11.16 points) from our effective purchase price of 81.40. The bad news in using this method is that although we saved 11.16 points compared to buying the stock at 92.56, if the stop-loss price is hit, we will still lose money on the trade ($1116). The good news is that we will still come out ahead of where we would have been if we had bought the stock at 92.56 initially.

Position Management

- Hold the position until the option expires or the stock is put to us at $85 a share.
- If the stock is put to us at effective price of 81.40 (85 − 3.60), we will have saved 11.16 a share (92.56 − 81.40). We will risk this amount on the trade and place a stop at 70.24.

Trade Result

Between the time this trade was entered and April option expiration, the price of IBM rallied sharply. As a result, the April 85 put option expired worthless (Figure 17.4).

Profit = $360

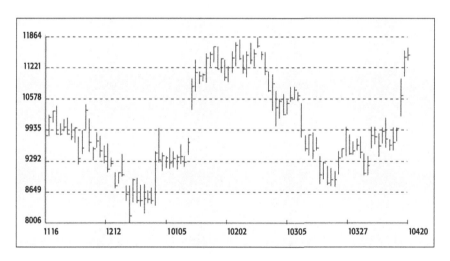

Figure 17.4   IBM rallies, put option expires worthless.

Chapter 18

WRITE A COVERED CALL

PURPOSE: To use time decay or high option volatility to hedge and/or generate income from an existing position.

Key Factors

1. You have some reason to expect the underlying to pause.
2. Option volatility is high.
3. You can take advantage of time decay by selling out-of-the-money options.

Options offer traders a number of unique opportunities. One opportunity they offer—particularly to longer-term investors—is the ability to hedge existing positions in an underlying security. If a trader is holding a position in a particular stock or futures market and wants to hedge that position, options are often the easiest and most effective alternative for achieving this objective. The most popular and commonly used hedging strategy is known as covered call writing. A covered call write involves writing a call option against a long position in the underlying security.

Although it is a popular strategy, covered call writing is probably the most commonly misused option-trading strategy. Most traders never consider writing covered calls until it is suggested to them by a broker. Once they do, they rarely stop to consider the reward and risk ramifications. At best, writing a covered call allows a trader to generate income from an existing position and to obtain some downside protection. At worst, this strategy limits your upside potential and provides only a limited amount of downside protection.

There are a number of different ways to use this strategy. For instance, some traders buy a stock they consider oversold and simultaneously write a call option against that position. This is generally referred to as a buy-write and is employed by an investor who is focused on total return (gain or loss on stock plus option premium collected). The method presented in this chapter differs slightly from that approach in that it involves writing call options against stocks (or futures contracts) that are already held, based on a given set of circumstances that we will discuss.

Covered calls should be written only when implied option volatility is high. This allows you to sell expensive options and to maximize the amount of premium you collect. Remember, writing a covered call affords you only a limited amount of downside protection and limits the amount of your upside potential. The higher the implied volatility, the more time premium an option writer can collect; therefore, the more downside protection he or she is afforded. Because of these factors you should only use this strategy when you can obtain a substantial amount of premium.

Covered call writing is not a market-timing strategy per se. It simply gives an investor the opportunity to take advantage of high option volatility and time decay. The way to take maximum advantage of time decay is to write out-of-the-money call options (which will likely expire worthless) when implied volatility is high.

The example trade in this chapter involves the stock of Computer Associates (symbol: CA).

1. In the graph in Figure 18.1 you can see that CA stock rallied 91% in just 11 trading days and then fell back below a long-term resistance level.
2. Figure 18.2 shows that the relative volatility rank is 10, indicating that CA options are expensive, thus signaling a favorable time to write options on this security.

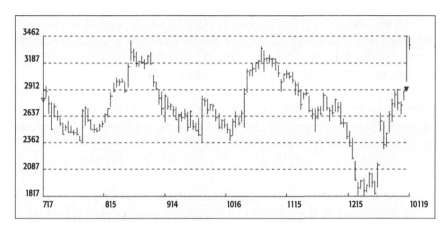

Figure 18.1 Computer Associates rallies sharply.

Given these two key elements, investors holding CA stock may consider writing a covered call if they expect the stock's price advance to pause. In selecting an expiration month and strike price to write, look for an option with a delta of 50 or less (i.e., at least slightly out of the money) and less than 60 days left until expiration.

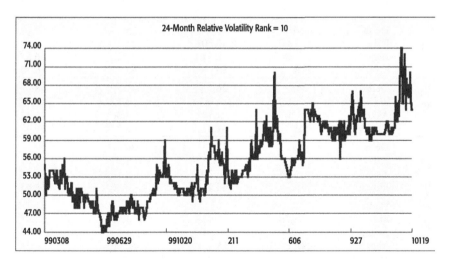

Figure 18.2 Computer Associates' implied volatility soars.

In the option grid in Table 18.1, you can see that we elected to write the February 35 call. This option has a delta of 48 and only 29 days left until expiration. Writing this option for 2.5 points gives us $250 of downside protection.

There is a right time and a wrong time to write a covered call against a given security. To enjoy the benefits of this strategy, it is important to recognize the most opportune times to use it and to act when the opportunity arises.

To maximize your potential when writing a covered call,

- Use this strategy when implied option volatility is very high (to maximize the amount of premium you receive when writing an option)

Table 18.1 Computer Associates Call Options

		Calls			
		JAN 0	**FEB** 28	**MAY** 120	**AUG** 211
30	Delta	100	73	70	70
	Bid	3.50	5.00	7.12	8.50
	Asked	3.88	5.37	7.62	9.00
	Imp. V.	NA	82.83	69.84	66.04
35	Delta	0	48	55	59
	Bid	.00	2.50	4.75	6.37
	Asked	.06	2.81	5.12	6.87
	Imp. V.	NA	85.05	68.43	66.70
40	Delta	0	26	41	48
	Bid	.00	1.00	3.12	4.75
	Asked	.06	1.18	3.50	5.12
	Imp. V.	NA	81.37	68.77	66.47
45	Delta	0	12	30	39
	Bid	.00	.31	1.93	3.50
	Asked	.06	.50	2.18	3.87
	Imp. V.	NA	80.16	66.90	66.48
50	Delta	0	5	21	31
	Bid	.00	.06	1.18	2.43
	Asked	.06	.31	1.37	2.75
	Imp. V.	NA	NA	66.00	64.59

- Sell call options with a delta no greater than 50 (i.e., sell an out-of-the-money call to maximize the beneficial effects of time decay)
- Sell options with no more than 60 (and preferably fewer) days until expiration
- Use this strategy after a security you are holding has experienced a significant rally and you expect it to consolidate or decline in the near term

In sum, if a security you are holding has experienced a sharp advance in price and implied volatility rises to a very high level, thus inflating the amount of premium available to option writers, you may benefit from writing a covered call.

The graph in Figure 18.3 depicts risk curves for three dates leading up to option expiration. While holding long 100 shares of CA, and with CA trading at 33.69, we sold one February 35 call option at a price of 2.50 (thus collecting $250 in premium).

The advantage of making this trade is that the $250 we receive for writing this option is ours to keep. As a result, the break-even point on our stock position (from this point forward) is reduced from 33.69 (if we were just holding the stock) to 31.39.

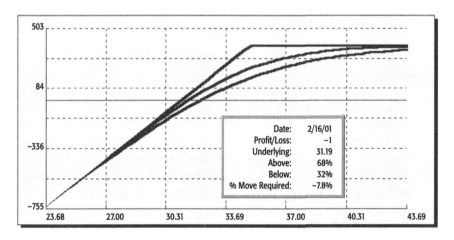

Figure 18.3 Computer Associates covered call risk curves.

To put it another way, we have 7.8% of downside protection. When the option was written, the probability of CA trading at or above this price at February option expiration was 65%. The disadvantage of writing a covered call is that it limits upside potential. If CA is trading above 35 at the time the February options expire the most that we can make on this trade is $380, regardless of how high the stock might rally.

You are limiting your upside potential while receiving only a limited amount of downside protection. This is an important factor that most traders never consider when writing covered calls.

Following the guidelines set out earlier for this strategy:

- We chose a stock with high option volatility (a relative volatility rank of 10) that was overbought.
- We sold a call option with a delta of less than 50 (the February 35 call has a delta of 48).
- We sold a call option with less than 60 days until expiration (the February options have 28 days left until expiration).

Position Taken

Long 100 shares of CA
Sell 1 February 35 call at 2.50.

In deciding how to manage a covered call position, you must address two risks:

1. *The first risk is that the stock may fall by more than the amount received when the call option was written.* Once that happens, the covered call provides no additional protection, so the potential loss becomes unlimited. (Technically, the risk is not unlimited since the stock can only go to zero, but the point is that beyond a certain price, the call option offers no additional protection.)
2. *The second risk is that the stock may rally sharply, causing the option that we wrote to trade in the money.* Once the option trades in the money, there is a possibility that the holder

of the option may exercise the option and our stock will be called away. If we do not want to give up our stock position, we must plan to buy back the call if the stock price rises.

Before writing a covered call, you must decide what you will do if the stock drops sharply or rallies sharply. If the stock drops sharply, your choices are these:

- Sell the stock, buy back the call, and exit the trade completely to avoid additional losses.
- Hold onto both positions and hope the stock bounces back.
- *Roll down.* Rolling down involves buying back the call option written initially and selling a new call option with a lower strike price. This is something of an advanced technique and will not be covered in detail here.

If the stock rallies sharply, you may do one of three things:

1. Let the stock be called away.
2. Buy back the call option you wrote (possibly at a higher price, thus incurring a loss).
3. Buy back the call option you wrote (possibly at a loss) and sell another further-out-of-the-money call option.

There are no absolute right or wrong answers for these decisions. Deciding whether to buy back the call or to let the stock be called away may depend on a number of factors. If you definitely want to hold the stock, or if you have a large gain and do not want to sell the stock, thus realizing a taxable capital gain, you will buy back the call option, more than likely paying a higher price than you sold it for originally. If you want, you can write another call with a higher strike price at that time. Although some traders like to think of covered call writing as "free money," you are essentially trading upside potential for a limited amount of downside protection. If the underlying security starts to rally and you buy back the call at a loss, the net effect is that your position-protecting, income-producing hedge ends up generating a loss.

For this example, we chose to let the stock be called away if the stock rallied above 35 and the option was exercised against us. On the downside, we entered a stop-loss to sell the stock at 29. A drop in this price would require a drop back into the previous trading range and would be a signal to us that the recent breakout had failed. If our stop-loss price for the stock is hit, we will simultaneously buy back the call option to avoid holding a short naked call position. Remember that holding a naked short call exposes you to unlimited risk.

Position Management

Stop-loss: Sell the stock and buy back the call option if the stock drops below 29.

Profit-taking: If the stock rises, hold until option expiration or until the stock is called away.

As shown in Figure 18.4, CA stock failed to follow through to the upside and drifted sideways to slightly higher through February option expiration. At the close of trading on option-expiration day, the stock was trading at 35.90. As a result, the 35 call was 0.90 point in the money. If we did not buy this call back before

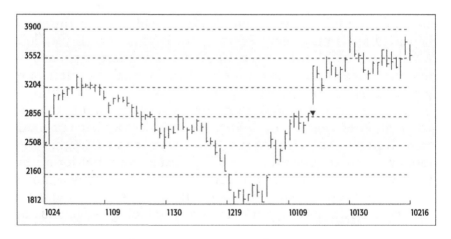

Figure 18.4   Computer Associates at February option expiration.

the close of trading, it would automatically be exercised by the Options Clearing Corporation and our stock would be called away. If we had wanted to continue to hold the stock, we would have to buy back the call before the close of trading on that day.

In this example, writing a covered call helped us achieve the best of both worlds. The stock rose from 33.69 to 35.90, generating a profit of $221. At the same time, the February 35 call lost all of its time premium and declined in price from 2.50 to 0.90 at expiration, generating another profit of $160 to the writer of this option (Table 18.2).

The end result is that as of February option expiration we have a profit of $380 and would still be holding our stock position if we bought back the call just before expiration. If we held the option through expiration, our stock position would be called away because our short option is in the money, thus triggering automatic exercise.

Table 18.2 Computer Associates Covered Call Result

Long/Short	Quantity	Type	Price In	Last Price	$ + /–
Long	100	Shares	33.69	35.90	+$221
Short	1	February 35 call	2.50	0.90	+$160

Trade Result

Option expired at 0.90 on February 16.
Stock closed at 35.90.

KEY POINT

Covered call writing should be considered only when implied volatility is high. Sell only out-of-the-money call options to maximize the effects of time decay.

Writing Covered Calls without Limiting Upside Potential

As you can see in Figure 18.5, the primary negative associated with writing covered calls against your entire underlying position is that you put yourself into a trade that has unlimited downside risk and only limited profit potential. If the stock you are holding collapses, you stand to take a large loss, reduced somewhat by the option premium you collected. If, however, the underlying security surprises you by advancing far more than you expected, you will not participate in any profit above the strike price of the option you wrote. Once the stock price exceeds the strike price for the option you wrote, for every point you make on the underlying you lose a point on the short call. Figure 18.5 shows the same CA trade highlighted earlier in this chapter using 1000 shares of stock and 10 covered call options. Note that above the strike price of 35, the profit is fixed. If the stock were to rally to 43.69, the writer of 10 covered calls would earn a maximum profit of $3866.

There is a way around the limited-profit-potential conundrum that offers the benefits of covered call writing while al-

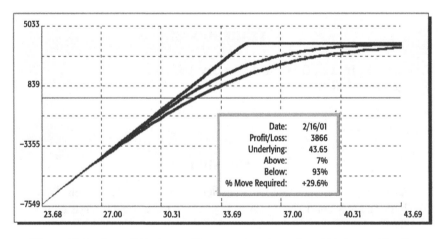

	Date:	2/16/01
Profit/Loss:	3866
Underlying:	43.65
Above:	7%
Below:	93%
% Move Required:	+29.6%

Figure 18.5   Long 1000 shares of Computer Associates, short 10 February 35 calls.

lowing you to participate in favorable movement by the underlying: Simply avoid writing covered calls in a 1:1 ratio. In other words, if you are holding 1000 shares of stock, you might consider writing 8 call options (or any number less than 10) instead of 10. By doing so, you still take in option premium, which offers you some downside protection and the opportunity to earn extra income. In addition, if the underlying security rallies sharply, although some of your position will likely be called away, you still retain a position in the underlying security.

Figure 18.6 shows the same CA trade highlighted earlier in this chapter using 1000 shares of stock, but only 8 covered-call options. Note that the profit on this trade continues to rise as the stock price advances. If the stock were to rally to 43.69, the writer of 8 covered calls would have a profit of $5020, and this profit would continue to grow as the stock advances.

From the perspective of a long-term strategy, writing less than the full number of options possible against your underlying position offers an attractive reward-to-risk tradeoff.

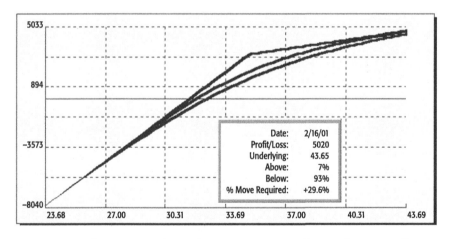

Figure 18.6   Long 1000 shares of Computer Associates, short 8 February 35 calls.

Chapter 19

ENTER A BUTTERFLY SPREAD

PURPOSE: To take advantage of high volatility and trading range conditions to collect option premium.

Key Factors

1. You have some reason to expect the underlying to stay in a trading range.
2. Option volatility is high (the higher, the better).
3. Less than 60 days remain until expiration.
4. You can enter the spread at a favorable price.

The butterfly spread strategy using calls involves buying a call option at one strike price, writing two calls at a higher strike price, and buying one more call at an even higher strike price. The butterfly spread strategy using puts involves buying a put option at one strike, writing two puts at a lower strike, and buying one more put at an even lower strike price. This trade is always done in a ratio of 1:2:1. In other words, you may enter the spread in a ratio of 1:2:1, 2:4:2, 3:6:3, 5:10:5, 10:20:10, and so on. From a strictly mathematical viewpoint, the butterfly spread can offer a very high probability of making money on any given trade.

A butterfly spread is a very specialized type of trade. Many traders learn about this strategy, try it a time or two, fail to make much money or actually lose money, and never try it again. To succeed with this strategy, you must understand the right circumstances for using it and then act decisively when the opportunity arises.

These are the key elements to look for when selecting butterfly spreads:

- *Choose an underlying security that is trading in a range with meaningful support and resistance points.* Once a butterfly spread is entered, the ideal scenario is for the underlying to remain relatively unchanged. Before entering a butterfly spread on a given security, look at a daily or weekly bar chart and see if you can easily identify meaningful support and resistance levels below and above the current price of the underlying. In other words, you want to find a security that appears to be in a trading range. This clearly involves some subjective analysis and there is of course no guarantee that the security will remain in a trading range. However, the main point is that if you find that the security you are considering is trending strongly or has just broken out to a new high or low, it is probably a poor candidate for this strategy.
- *Implied option volatility is high.* When you are considering a butterfly spread, option volatility should be as high as possible. This strategy makes money from having the middle strike price (i.e., the option you write) lose time premium. In other words, the more time premium built into the price of the option you write, the greater your profit potential. Therefore, the way to maximize your profit potential is to focus on securities with high option volatility.
- *No more than 60 days remain until option expiration.* By writing options when volatility is high, we hope to profit from a decline in volatility. We also can add time decay to our arsenal by writing options that do not have much time left until expiration. Ideally, you will enter butterfly spreads using options with 30 days or less until expiration. As a rule of thumb, you should not go out more than 60 days.
- *Sell at-the-money or slightly out-of-the-money options.* This is more of a guideline than a rule, but ideally you should look to write an option that is at the money or one strike price out of the money. Writing an out-of-the-money option gives you

a greater chance of collecting premium via time decay than writing an in-the-money option that has intrinsic value. Intrinsic value in an option will dissipate only if the underlying security moves far enough to push that particular option out of the money. In addition, you do not want to sell an option that is far out of the money, otherwise the underlying security must make a move in that direction to generate a profit. A butterfly spread is a neutral position, and you don't want to enter a position in which the underlying must move very far in a given direction for you to profit. If you really expect the underlying to move substantially in a given direction, the butterfly spread strategy is a poor choice.

Many traders make one or more critical mistakes when trading butterfly spreads, such as:

- Using market orders to buy or sell the individual options used in the spread
- Putting the trade on and then checking back near expiration to see how the trade is working out
- Paying too much in commissions

The good news about butterfly spreads is that if you are able to enter and exit them at a favorable price, your probability of generating a profit is very high. When entering a butterfly spread, it is usually essential to use a limit order to be certain that you enter the position at a price that makes the trade worth taking in the first place. The bad news is that because this strategy has limited profit potential, if you are forced to exit the trade earlier than expected, you may not be able to obtain a favorable price. Exiting a butterfly spread at the market could eat up all or part of your potential profit.

Commissions are also a major consideration with this strategy. In a butterfly spread you are trading three different options. If you are paying retail commissions on three separate options to enter the trade and again to exit the trade, it is quite possible that commissions alone could eat up all your profit potential. Before using this strategy, be certain to ask your broker how much you will pay in commissions to enter and exit the trade.

In Figure 19.1 you can see that as of January 5, implied volatility on Intel options was extremely high. In Figure 19.2 you can identify support and resistance levels for the price of Intel stock at 29.81 and 47.15, respectively. This suggests that Intel may be a good candidate for a butterfly spread. With Intel trading at 32.06, we see in Table 19.1 that we can sell the at-the-money 32.5 February option as the middle option in a butterfly spread. We want to buy 1 February 27.5 call and 1 February 37.5 call for every 2 February 32.5 calls we write. If we can enter this spread at current market prices, we will enter the trade at a net delta of 0, indicating a trade that is almost exactly neutral. The market prices for the 27.5 call, the 32.5 call, and the 37.5 call are 5.75, 3.06, and 1.19, respectively. On a 1:2:1 spread, the net debit (i.e., the amount we would pay to enter the spread) would be (5.75 – (3.06 × 2) – 1.19), or 0.8125, or \$81.25. If we want to do a 5:10:5 butterfly spread at this price, we would need to place the following order with the broker:

I want to enter a spread order as follows: This is a day order [Do not place open orders to enter a butterfly spread. The underlying might make a huge move by tomorrow, and a spread that is neutral today may be far

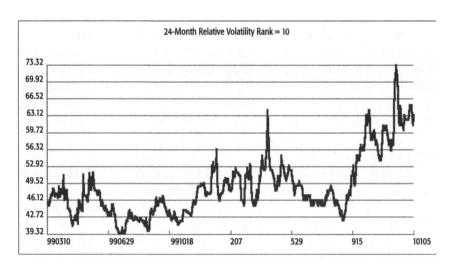

Figure 19.1   Intel option volatility is at the high end of its historic range.

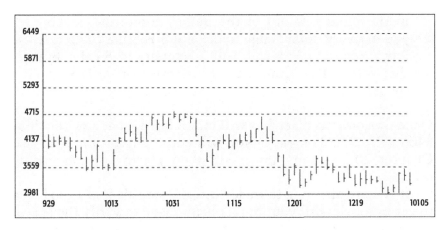

Figure 19.2 Intel has identifiable support (29.81) and resistance (47.15) levels.

Table 19.1 Establish a Butterfly Spread Using Intel Calls

		Calls			
		JAN 14	FEB 42	APR 106	JUL 197
25	Price	7.38	8.00	9.12	10.38
	Delta	95	88	81	79
	Imp. V.	100.05	78.05	70.12	67.31
27.5	Price	5.25	5.75	7.12	8.75
	Delta	85	78	74	73
	Imp. V.	87.81	73.15	69.62	64.66
30	Price	3.25	4.38	5.88	7.38
	Delta	69	66	65	66
	Imp. V.	83.26	73.40	68.58	63.40
32.5	Price	1.88	3.06	4.75	6.12
	Delta	50	53	57	60
	Imp. V.	80.37	71.80	67.20	62.45
35	Price	1.00	2.00	3.50	5.00
	Delta	32	41	49	53
	Imp. V.	78.83	71.23	66.59	61.88
37.5	Price	.44	1.19	2.75	4.00
	Delta	18	30	41	47
	Imp. V.	80.27	67.73	65.62	61.11

in the money or out of the money tomorrow, leaving you in a very unfavorable trade.] Buy 1 February 27.5 call. Buy 1 February 37.5 call. Sell 2 February 32.5 calls. Buy this spread five times at a limit price of 0.8125 per spread.

Once this order is placed, it will either be filled at a net debit of $406 ($81.25 × 5) or less or you will enter no position at all (see Chapter 20 for more information on placing option-trading orders).

If you are planning to trade butterfly spreads it is a good idea to get in touch with your broker beforehand to verify the appropriate procedure for entering this type of spread order and the commissions involved. If your broker does not know what a butterfly spread is, get another broker for your option trading.

The graph in Figure 19.3 depicts risk curves for five dates leading up to option expiration. With Intel trading at 32.06, we purchased 5 February 27.5 calls at 5.75, sold 10 February 32.5 calls at 3.06, and bought 5 February 37.5 calls at 1.19. The total dollar risk associated with this trade is equal to the amount of premium paid to buy the options, or $406 in this case.

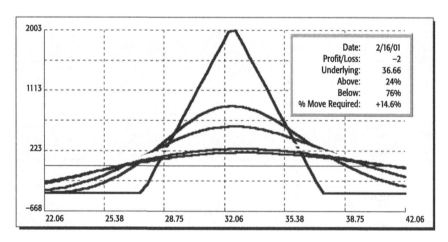

Figure 19.3   Intel butterfly spread risk curves.

The risk curve lines in the graph in Figure 19.3 clearly depict the positive effect of time decay that will occur if Intel stays within its current range. There is a tradeoff involved: Initially the range of profitability is quite wide, but as expiration draws closer, the goods news is that the maximum potential profit rises each week. The bad news is that the range of underlying prices that will result in a profit grows narrower each week. This is simply a function of time decay.

Many traders look at the risk curves for a butterfly spread and become mesmerized by the maximum potential profit at expiration. This is a mistake.

This profit will be obtained only if the underlying closes on option-expiration day at exactly the middle strike price. The odds of this happening are extremely slim and not worth playing for.

As indicated on the graph (Figure 19.3), if we were to hold this position until option expiration, our break-even prices are 28.30 on the downside and 36.70 on the upside. If we are still holding this position near expiration and Intel is not trading outside of that range, this trade should show a profit. When the trade was entered, there was a 25% probability that Intel would be below 28.30 at expiration and a 27% probability that Intel would be above 36.70. Statistically, there is a 50% probability that Intel would be between the two break-even points of 28.30 and 36.70 at option expiration.

The primary risk involved with the butterfly spread is that the underlying security will make a significant price move before option expiration, thus leaving it outside your break-even points.

Position Taken

Buy 5 February 27.5 calls at 5.75.
Sell 10 February 32.5 calls at 3.06.
Buy 5 February 37.5 calls at 1.19.

Maximum risk	–$406
Net delta	10
Days to expiration	42
Probability of profit	47%
Current underlying price	32.06
Break-even price at expiration	Above 28.30 and below 36.70

In theory the maximum risk on this trade is $406. In the worst-case scenario (i.e., if Intel rallies or declines sharply and is trading below 27.5 or above 37.5 at expiration), we can in theory hold this trade until expiration and lose no more than that amount. However, with a butterfly spread it can be a little more complicated than that. If Intel is trading below 27.5 at expiration, all the options in our spread will expire worthless. No follow-up action is needed, and we would take a loss of $406.

At any price above 27.5, however, follow-up action may be needed before expiration. To understand why follow-up action may be needed, consider the following scenarios:

- If we hold this trade through expiration and Intel closes at 30, our 5 27.5 calls will automatically be exercised and, come the following Monday morning, we will be long 500 shares of Intel stock at a cost of $13,750 (5 calls × 27.5 × $100).
- If we hold this trade through expiration and Intel closes at 35, our 5 27.5 calls will automatically be exercised, as will our 10 short 32.5 calls. Come the following Monday morning, we will be short 500 shares of Intel stock with the appropriate margin requirement due to maintain this position.
- If we hold this trade through expiration and Intel closes at 40, all our options from this trade will automatically be exercised and will offset each other, leaving us with no position in the underlying.

The real danger here occurs about 10 minutes before the close of trading on option-expiration day. If the stock is trading at 27.25 just before expiration, a trader might assume that he does not need to be concerned about any exercise or assignment complications. However, if the stock rallies 1.00 in the final 10 minutes of trading and closes at 28.25, the trader will be assigned on the 27.5 calls. The bottom line is that if we do not want to assume a position in the underlying security, we must plan on exiting this trade before expiration. And therein lies another complication.

Because we are buying and selling three different options, if we were to simply close each position at the market, chances are that the bid-ask spreads would eat up much, if not all, our potential profit. Similarly, if we place a limit order to get out of the spread at a certain amount, there is a chance we might not get filled at all. This potentially tricky situation is one of the reasons we described butterfly spreads as a specialized strategy.

There are no magic formulas for determining when to exit a butterfly spread. What is important is to have a plan for exiting the trade when you enter the trade. One useful rule of thumb is to plan to exit the trade before expiration at the first good opportunity. We define a good opportunity as a situation in which the underlying security is trading between our break-even points and volatility has fallen enough, or time decay has worked enough in our favor, to generate an acceptable open profit. At that point we take what profit we can from this trade and move on.

We will also set in place two other contingency plans:

1. If Intel falls in price and the amount of time premium in the February 32.5 calls that we wrote drops to 0.25 or lower, we will close the entire trade.
2. If Intel rallies in price and the amount of time premium in the February 32.5 calls that we wrote falls to 0.125 points or less, we will exit the entire trade.

Contingency 1 is essentially a stop-loss measure. Although our risk is limited, if Intel falls far enough that our short option has almost no time premium left, it is basically a long shot to get back into our profitable range.

Contingency 2 is a measure designed to keep from getting assigned on the short option.

Barring the occurrence of contingency 1 or 2, we will wait to exit this trade at the first good opportunity. Looking again at Figure 19.1, you will see that in the past two years option volatility for Intel has ranged from a high of 73 to a low of 39. Figure 19.4 shows the expected return for this trade a week before expiration, depending on the level of volatility at that time. If the price of Intel is between the upper and lower strikes (27.5 and 37.5), the lower the volatility, the higher the maximum profit potential.

If Intel is unchanged a week before expiration and volatility falls to its previous low of 39, we would expect this trade to show an open profit of approximately $1386. This possibility is shown by the uppermost line, which peaks in the middle of the graph in Figure 19.4. Conversely, if Intel is unchanged a week before expiration and volatility rises to its previous high of 73, we would expect this trade to show an open profit of approximately $868. This possibility is shown by the bottom line, which peaks in the middle of the graph.

It would be extremely optimistic to assume that the stock will be unchanged *and* that volatility will fall to its previous low. Therefore, we decide arbitrarily that if we can close out the entire trade with a profit of $500 or more, we will do so when that opportunity arises.

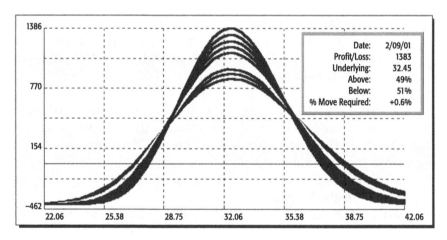

Figure 19.4   Intel butterfly spread risk curves for February 9, assuming different volatility levels.

Remember, the higher the profit you strive to attain, the lower the probability that you will attain it.

Position Management

Stop-loss:

- Close trade if price of February 32.5 call drops to 0.25 or lower.
- Close trade if time premium left in February 32.5 call drops to 0.125.

Profit-taking: If the trade can be exited with a profit of $500 or more before expiration, close the trade.

As you can see in Table 19.2, this trade worked out well, generating a profit of $778 as of February 9, which was one week before option expiration. Figure 19.5 shows that Intel initially rallied above the upper strike price of 37.5. Had this rally continued, we would have had to monitor the amount of time premium in the February 32.5 call on a daily basis to avoid getting into a situation in which the option we had sold short might be exercised, thus throwing our trade out of whack. If we get assigned on our short position, we would have to buy 1000 shares of Intel at the market and deliver them at a price of 32.5 a share. We would still be left holding 5 27.5 calls and 5 37.5 calls. This would be a far different situation than the one we intended to be in when we originally entered this butterfly spread.

Fortunately, that rally did not follow through and the stock fell back near the middle strike price, thus allowing time decay

Table 19.2 Intel Butterfly Spread Results

Long/Short	Quantity	Type	Price In	Last Price	$ + /–
Long	5	February 27.5 call	5.75	5.88	+$63
Short	10	February 32.5 call	3.06	1.81	+$1248
Long	5	February 37.5 call	1.19	.13	–$533

on the February 32.5 calls to begin working in our favor. Also helping out was the fact that Intel option volatility dropped from 60 to 50 during this time, as you can see in Figure 19.6. This, too, helped eat away at the amount of time premium in the at-the-money options that we wrote.

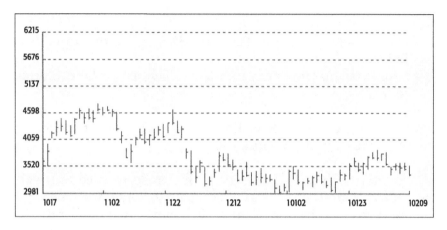

Figure 19.5   Intel stock price stays in a range.

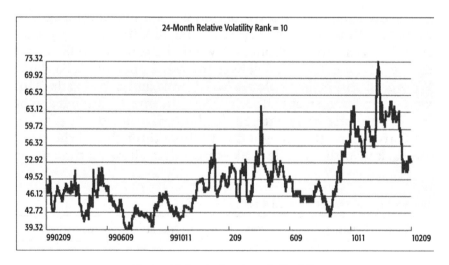

Figure 19.6   Intel option volatility falls.

Trade Result

Open profit taken on February 9.

Profit = $778

KEY POINT

The way to make money with a butterfly spread is to have the underlying security remain in a narrow range or for volatility to decline. When looking to trade a butterfly spread, stick to underlying securities whose options are currently trading at a very high level of volatility. Look for obvious support and resistance levels above and below the current price of the underlying security.

In exiting a butterfly spread, it often pays to look for the first good opportunity to exit with a satisfactory profit and move on to the next trade.

Chapter 20

PLACING TRADES

Once you gain an understanding of the important concepts related to trading options and have decided on the strategy or strategies to employ, you must cross the line into the real world of trading. Unfortunately, many traders underestimate the amount of time and work involved in trading options. Once you have updated any necessary data, conducted your analysis, and selected the trade or trades that you want to enter or exit, you must place the appropriate order with your broker to execute that trade.

Order placement is a critical issue since mistakes can result in serious losses. Complicating the matter is the fact that placing option orders can be much more complex than buying or selling a stock or futures contract. Different brokers use different terminology and protocol when placing option orders, particularly option spread orders. One other potential problem is that many brokers who deal with options only on an as-needed basis are not as familiar with the process as you may need them to be.

The advent of the Internet has created an opportunity for independent traders to trade on-line rather than having to call a broker and place orders over the phone. Some traders see this as an advantage; others would still prefer to place their orders with an actual person rather than on-line.

Considerations in Placing Option Orders

Whenever you plan to place an option order, there are a number of possible considerations, including these:

- Are you going to place an order to buy or sell a single option?
- Do you plan to enter into or exit a spread or a straddle?
- Do you want to place a day order, or should your order be placed as good till canceled (GTC)?
- Are you going to enter or exit the trade at the market?
- Do you plan to enter or exit the trade at a limit price?
- Do you know the symbol for the option you are planning to trade?

With a live broker you can usually just name the stock itself when placing an order. For example, with most live brokers, placing a phone order to buy 10 Microsoft April 50 calls is sufficient. However, when entering orders on-line, you generally need the actual option root symbol for each option you want to trade. For example, the symbol for Microsoft stock is MSFT, but the symbol for Microsoft options is MSQ. With many online brokers, if you tried to buy an MSFT option, you might get an error message telling you that the symbol is not valid. In this example, you would need to enter the symbol MSQ when placing the trade.

Placing Orders by Phone and On-line

Generally there is a different protocol for entering orders over the phone to a live broker than entering orders on-line. As you will see in the examples in this chapter, a live broker wants you to place the order using a particular format each time to facilitate getting the order entered with no mistakes. Most on-line brokers provide an onscreen order placement form (or forms). You can fill in the required information in any order you want just so long as you provide all the necessary information before you actually submit the order.

Buy Naked Calls or Puts (Chapter 12)

The trade discussed in Chapter 12 involved buying 2 JDS Uniphase put options and then selling them one at a time. "Day order—buy to open 2 JDS Uniphase March 65 puts at the market."

- To enter the trade on-line, see Figure 20.1.
- To take a profit on one option by phone: "Day order—sell to close 1 JDS Uniphase March 65 put at the market."
- To take a profit on one option on-line, see Figure 20.2.
- To exit the trade by phone: "Day order—sell to close 1 JDS Uniphase March 65 put at the market."
- To cxit thc tradc on-linc, scc Figure 20.3.

Figure 20.1   Entry order for JDS Uniphase March 65 puts.
(*Source:* All screen shots in Chapter 20 appear courtesy of Mr. Stock.)

Figure 20.2   Exit 1 JDS Uniphase March 65 put.

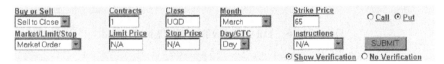

Figure 20.3   Exit 1 JDS Uniphase March 65 put.

Buy a Backspread (Chapter 13)

The trade discussed in Chapter 13 involved selling five call options at one strike price and buying 11 call options at a higher strike price. "Day order—buy to open 11 Toys "R" Us June 17 and a half calls at the market" and "Day order—sell to open 5 Toys "R" Us June 12 and a half calls at the market."

- To enter the trades on-line, see Figures 20.4 and 20.5.
- To exit the trade by phone: "Day Order—buy to close 5 Toys "R" Us June 12 and a half calls at the market" and "Day Order—sell to close 11 Toys "R" Us June 17 and a half calls at the market."
- To exit the trade on-line, see Figures 20.6 and 20.7.

Figure 20.4   Entry order for Toys "R" Us backspread.

Figure 20.5   Entry order for Toys "R" Us backspread.

Figure 20.6   Exit order for Toys "R" Us backspread.

Figure 20.7   Exit order for Toys "R" Us backspread.

Buy a Calendar Spread (Chapter 14)

The trade discussed in Chapter 14 involved buying 10 April, 50 AOL call options and selling 10 February AOL call options. "I want to place a spread order."

- To enter the trade *at the market* on-line, see Figure 20.8.
- To enter the trade *at a limit price* by phone: "I want to place a spread order with a limit price. Part 1: Day order—buy to open 1 America Online April 50 put. Part 2: Day order—sell to open 1 America Online February 50 put. Buy the spread 10 times at a limit price of 1.95 points."
- To enter the trade *at a limit price* on-line, see Figure 20.9.
- To exit the trade by phone: "I want to place a spread order. Part 1: Day order—buy to close 1 America Online February 50 put. Part 2: Day order—sell to close 1 America Online April 50 put. Sell the spread 10 times at the market."
  To exit the trade on-line, see Figure 20.10.

Figure 20.8 Entry order for America Online calendar spread.

Figure 20.9 Entry order for America Online calendar spread.

Figure 20.10 Exit order for America Online calendar spread.

Buy a Straddle (Chapter 15)

The trade discussed in Chapter 15 involved buying the April 40 call and the April 40 put for Reader's Digest. "I want to place an order to enter a long straddle. Day order—buy the Reader's Digest April 40 straddle six times at the market."

- To enter the trade *at the market* on-line, See Figure 20.11.
- To enter the trade *at a limit price* by phone: "I want to place an order to enter a long straddle. Day Order—buy to open the Reader's Digest April 40 straddle six times at a limit price of 5.62 points."
- To enter the trade *at a limit price* on-line, See Figure 20.12.
- To exit the trade by phone: "I want to place a straddle order. Day Order—sell to close the Reader's Digest April 40 straddle six times at the market."
- To exit the trade on-line, see Figure 20.13.

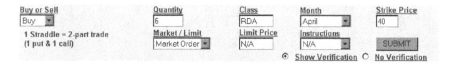

Figure 20.11   Entry order for Reader's Digest straddle.

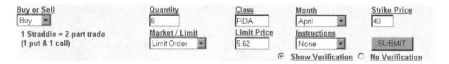

Figure 20.12   Entry order for Reader's Digest straddle.

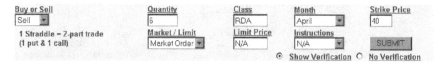

Figure 20.13   Exit order for Reader's Digest straddle.

Sell a Vertical Spread (Chapter 16)

The trade discussed in Chapter 16 involved selling IBM February 80 puts and buying February 75 puts. "I want to place a spread order with a limit price. Part 1: Buy to open 1 IBM February 75 put. Part 2: Sell to open 1 IBM February 80 put. Sell the spread six times at a limit price of 1.25 points."

- To enter the trade *at a limit price* on-line, see Figure 20.14.
- To exit the trade by phone: "I want to place a spread order. Part 1: Day order—sell to close 1 IBM February 75 put. Part 1: Day order—buy to close 1 IBM February 80 put. Buy the spread six times at the market."
- To exit the trade on-line, see Figure 20.15.

Figure 20.14 Entry order for IBM vertical spread.

Figure 20.15 Exit order for IBM vertical spread.

Sell a Naked Put (Chapter 17)

The trade discussed in Chapter 17 involved selling an IBM April 85 put. "Day order—sell to open 1 IBM April 85 put at the market."
- To enter the trade *at the market* on-line, see Figure 20.16.
- To enter the trade *at a limit price* by phone: "Day order—sell to open 1 IBM April 85 put at a limit price of 3.60 points."

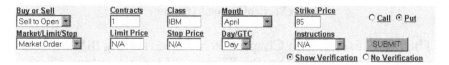

Figure 20.16   Entry order for IBM naked put.

- To enter the trade *at a limit price* on-line, See Figure 20.17.
- To exit the trade by phone: "Day order—buy to close 1 IBM April 85 put at the market."
- To exit the trade on-line, see Figure 20.18.

Figure 20.17   Entry order for IBM naked put.

Figure 20.18   Exit order for IBM naked put.

Write a Covered Call (Chapter 18)

The following orders assume that you are already long 100 shares of Computer Associates stock.

The trade discussed in Chapter 18 involved selling one Computer Associates February 35 call option, based on the assumption that you are already long 100 shares of Computer Associates stock. "Day order—sell to open 1 Computer Associates February 25 call at the market."

- To enter the trade *at the market* on-line, see Figure 20.19.
- To enter the trade *at a limit price* by phone: "Day order—sell to open 1 Computer Associates February 25 call at a limit price of 2.50 points."
- To enter the trade *at a limit price* on-line, see Figure 20.20.

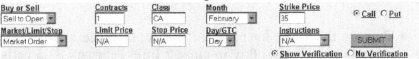

Figure 20.19 Entry order for Computer Associates covered call.

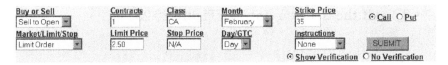

Figure 20.20 Entry order for Computer Associates covered call.

- To exit the trade by phone: "Day order—buy to close 1 Computer Associates February 25 call at the market."
- To exit the trade on-line, see Figure 20.21.

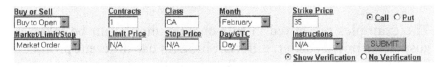

Figure 20.21 Exit order for Computer Associates covered call.

Buy a Butterfly Spread (Chapter 19)

The trade discussed in Chapter 19 involved buying Intel call options at 27.5 and 37.5 and selling the 32.5 strike. "I want to place a three-part spread order with a limit price. Part 1: Buy to open 1 Intel February 27.5 call. Part 2: Buy to open 1 Intel February 37.5 call. Part 3: Sell to open 2 Intel February 32.5 calls. Buy the spread five times at a limit price of thirteen-sixteenths."

- To enter the trade *at a limit price* on-line, see Figure 20.22.

Figure 20.22 Entry order for Intel butterfly spreads.

- To exit the trade by phone: "I want to place a three-part spread order. Part 1: Buy to close 2 Intel February 32.5 calls. Part 2: Sell to close one Intel February 27.5 call. Part 3: Sell to close one Intel February 37.5 call. Sell the spread 5 times at the market."
- To exit the trade on-line, see Figure 20.23.

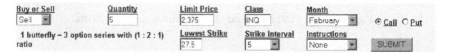

Figure 20.23   Exit order for Intel butterfly.

Summary

The examples presented in this chapter should not be taken as gospel. As noted earlier, different brokers use different protocols for option order placement. Before placing any option orders, double-check with your broker about format and wording that should be used for an order for any given trading strategy.

Epilogue

SOME RANDOM THOUGHTS FOR OPTION TRADERS

By now you should have some idea about what it takes to succeed in option trading. You should know that there are certain basic concepts that you must understand and apply properly if you hope to succeed in the long run. For example, until you understand and appreciate the impact of time decay and volatility on any option position you might consider, any success you enjoy in the short run is unlikely to last.

You should recognize that option trading can be significantly and fundamentally different from simply buying and selling stocks or futures contracts. A long stock position makes a point each time the stock rises a point and loses a point each time the stock falls a point. A given option position—depending on its makeup—might make a lot of money if the stock rises or falls, whereas another position will only make money if the stock does *not* rise or fall beyond a certain amount. Understanding how to craft a position to achieve a particular objective is what separates the professional option trader from the masses hoping to buy a cheap option and hit a home run.

No one succeeds in trading because they got lucky on a trade or two. Those who succeed consistently in the long run are those who make the effort and take the time to learn the skills required to achieve lasting success. They apply these lessons in the real world, trade after trade.

Real-world trading is a far different experience from paper trading or system development. Paper trading can be fun. System development can be intellectually stimulating. Trading in the real world with real money on the line can be downright frightening. There is a feeling you get in the pit of your stomach when things go very wrong that cannot be described. When the prospect of losing money—especially big money—raises its ugly head, emotion can take over and cause even the most rational trading veteran to throw the trading plan out the window and simply react in an effort to stop the pain. You should recognize by now the need to plan in advance for each trade's worst case scenario before getting into the trade.

One of the best things you can do right now is to narrow down the list of available option-trading strategies and determine which ones you will be most comfortable using. Too many traders dabble, trying a butterfly spread this week, a backspread the next, and so forth. This is no way to succeed.

You should also familiarize yourself with which strategies are best used in a given situation. Want to pick a bottom, but you're afraid of an outright collapse by the underlying? If volatility is low, consider a backspread. If volatility is high, consider selling a vertical spread, writing an option with a strike price below the recent low. Is a stock putting you to sleep, wandering in a narrow range between support and resistance? If volatility is low, consider a calendar spread. Think that it's due for a breakout? Consider buying a straddle. Itching to buy a particular stock but just can't pull the trigger? If volatility is high, consider selling a naked put. If volatility is low, consider buying a longer-term call option. Want to buy a call on a stock that you just know is going to rally, but option volatility is going through the roof? Consider buying a shorter-term, deep-in-the-money call option to minimize the amount of time premium you pay. The possibilities are endless.

You must also remember that getting into a trade is only one part of the equation. In fact, in many instances selecting and entering a trade is the easy part. Sometimes big trends play out and traders who cash out quickly miss out on big potential profits. At other times big profits on option trades exist for only a very short time and then vanish forever. For this reason it is absolutely critical to your long-term success that you determine when you enter each trade what criteria you will use to exit the trade. Without this type of planning, most traders are doomed to veering with each twist in the road.

Consistently applying the principles and concepts detailed in this book offers you the greatest opportunity for consistent, long-term success. I wish you good fortune in achieving that goal.

Appendix A

PROVEST OPTION TRADING METHOD CRITERIA

The PROVEST Option Trading Method: A Framework for Trade Selection

There are several key factors to consider in determining the best option-trading strategy to use at any given moment for a given underlying security. Selecting from the available strategies involves knowing what to look for in terms of probability, volatility, time to expiration, the skew of implied volatilities, and market movement. The PROVEST Option Trading Method was developed to identify specific criteria in each of these key areas. The primary factors and key considerations are detailed in Table A.1.

By defining appropriate PROVEST factors for each of the trading strategies, we create a structured approach to options trading. In turn, we can zero in on trades that generate the highest probability of making money, rather than relying on gut feel and luck in the marketplace (see Table A.2).

Table A.1   The PROVEST Option Trading Method

What It Is	Why It Matters
PRO is for probability	What is the probability that a given option will expire in the money? Should I buy or sell in-the-money or out-of-the-money options? The PROVEST method uses option deltas and the volatility of the underlying security to measure the probability that a given trade will generate a profit.
V is for volatility	Is implied option volatility currently high or low on a historic basis? That is, are options cheap (favoring option buyers) or expensive (favoring option writers)?
E is for expiration	How much time is left until expiration? Is my position helped or hurt by time decay?
S is for skew	Can I gain an edge by spreading cheap options rather than expensive options?
T is for timing	What market conditions should I look for before implementing a given strategy?

Table A.2 PROVEST Option Trading Method Summary Table

Strategy	Delta	Volatility	Expiration	Skew	Timing
Buy naked options	> 50; Buying in-the-money options is preferable. This reduces amount of time premium paid as a percent of option price and increases probability of profit.	The lower the better. The higher the volatility, the further in the money and the shorter term the option you buy should be.	Depends on trading time frame; must be careful during 2 weeks before expiration, as time decay accelerates.	Not relevant.	Only use when very bullish or very bearish.
Buy a backspread	Attempt to make trade delta neutral at time of entry; generally prefer to write slightly in-the-money options.	Lower is better. A rise in volatility can help a lot; a decline in volatility can hurt a lot.	Best to buy longer-term options to limit time decay while waiting for the underlying to move.	Higher volatility for option sold is a plus.	Use when looking for a move in a particular direction but not comfortable buying naked options.
Buy a calendar spread	Delta of 35 to 65, or no more than one strike out of the money.	The lower the better. A rise in volatility can help tremendously; a decline in volatility can be disastrous.	≤45 days.	Enter trade only if 15% higher volatility for option sold.	Look for meaningful support and resistance levels bounding a trading range.
Buy a straddle	Attempt to make trade delta neutral; you want an equal chance to make money if underlying rises or falls.	The lower the better. Reduces amount you pay, increases your probability of profit, and a rise in volatility can help.	74 days or more.	Not meaningful.	Look for extended consolidation (i.e., underlying is due for a trend.).

(continues)

253

Table A.2 PROVEST Option Trading Method Summary Table (*continued*)

Strategy	Delta	Volatility	Expiration	Skew	Timing
Sell a vertical spread	Calls: ≤ 40 Puts: ≥ –40 (i.e., sell out-of-the-money options).	The higher the better. The higher the volatility, the greater the profit potential.	≤ 60 days	Ideally a higher volatility for option sold.	Look for support (or resistance) between underlying price and strike price of option sold.
Sell naked puts	Delta > –50 (i.e. sell out-of-the-money options to take advantage of time decay).	Use only when volatility is extremely high.	≤ 60 days.	Not meaningful.	Best used when a stock you want to buy is oversold and volatility has exploded.
Write a covered call	≤ 40 for options sold (i.e., sell out-of-the-money options to take advantage of time decay).	Only write covered call when volatility is extremely high to maximize the amount of premium you collect.	≤ 60 days.	Not meaningful.	Best used when volatility is high and underlying security is overbought.
Butterfly spread	Sell slightly out-of-money option as middle strike of spread.	The higher, the better; trade makes money from time decay or a decline in volatility, or both.	≤ 60 days, ≤ 30 is even better.	Ideal if middle option (i.e., the one you write) is trading at a higher volatility than the options you buy.	Look for meaningful support and resistance.

Appendix B

OPTION EXCHANGES, OPTION BROKERS, OPTION SYMBOLS, AND OPTION VOLUME

Exchanges

Options are traded at each of the exchanges listed in Tables B.1 and B.2.

Table B.1 Stock and Stock Index Option Exchanges

Exchange	Web Site
Chicago Board Options Exchange (CBOE)	www.cboe.com
American Stock Exchange	www.options.nasdaq-amex.com
Philadelphia Stock Exchange	www.phlx.com
Pacific Stock Exchange	www.pacificex.com

Table B.2 Exchanges Trading Futures Options

Exchange	Web Site
Chicago Board of Trade	www.cbot.com
Chicago Mercantile Exchange	www.cme.com
COMEX (Metals)	www.nymex.com
New York Board of Trade	www.nybot.com
New York Mercantile Exchange (Energies)	www.nymex.com

255

Table B.3   Brokers Dealing in Stock and Stock Index Options

Firm	Web Site	Phone	Account Minimum	Commissions
A-1 Financial	www.a1financial.com	877-a1-financial	$1000	$23 + $2.50 per contract
Accutrade	www.accutrade.com	800-494-8949	$5000	$35; $1.5 to $8 per contract
Ameritrade	www.ameritrade	800-669-3900	$2000	$25+$1.75 per contract ($29 minimum)
Benjamin & Jerold	www.stockoptions.com	800-446-5112	$5000	$1.50 to $5.90 per contract ($36 minimum)
Brown & Co.	www.brownco.com	800-357-4410	$15,000	$15 + $1.50 per contract ($25 minimum)
CompuTEL Securities	www.computel.com	800-432-0327	$5000	$24 + $1 per contract
Dreyfus Brokerage Services	www.edreyfus.com	800-421-8395	$2000	$15 + $1.75 per contract
Mr. Stock	www.mrstock.com	800-470-1896	$2000	$14.95 + $1.50 per contract
Preferred Trade	www.preferredtrade.com	800-949-3504	$1000	$19.95, or $2.50 to $3.00 per contract
Quick & Reilly	www.quick-reilly.com	800-221-7220	None	$37.50 plus $1.75 per contract
Schwab OnLine	www.eschwab.com	800-435-4000	$2500	$35 + 1.75 per contract
Wall Street Access	www.wsaccess.com	800-925-5781	$10,000	$25 plus $1.50 to $2.50 per contract
Wall Street Electronica	www.wallstreete.com	888-925-5783	$2500 to $10,000	$25 plus $2.50 per contract

Brokerage Firms

Most brokerage firms offer you the capability of trading options, but not all firms offer the same level of commitment to option trading. Tables B.3 and B.4 present a short list of brokerage firms that offer option trading or even emphasize it.

Table B.4   Brokers Dealing in Futures Options

Firm	Web Site	Phone
Jack Carl	www.jackcarl.com	800-621-3424
Lind-Waldock	www.lind-waldock.com	800-445-2000
NetFutures	www.netfutures.com	800-872-6673
Peregrine Financial Group	www.pfg.com	800-333-5673
Professional Market Brokerage	www.pmbinc.com	800-672-2462
Robbins Trading	www.robbinstrading.com	800-453-4444
Zap Futures	www.zapfutures.com	800-441-1616

Resources

Other helpful sites can be found in Table B.5.

Table B.5

Firm	Web Site	What It Offers
Chicago Board Options Exchange (CBOE)	www.cboe.com	Exchange specific quotes, education, and strategies
Options Clearing Corporation	www.optionsclearing.com	Information from the company that clears executions for all exchanges
New Options	Onn.theocc.com/series/ pgms/todays_add.pl	Lists new options from the Options Clearing Corporation
Options Industry Council	www.optionscentral.com	AMEX, CBOE, PCX, and PHLX joined to create this educational site for option traders
Author's Company Web sites	www.essextrading.com www.essexcta.com	Various trading-related information

(continues)

Table B.5 (*continued*)

Firm	Web Site	What It Offers
Books on Trading	www.traderslibrary.com	Trading books and tapes
Web Investor Options Directory	www.thewebinvestor.com	Links to advisories, brokers, newsletters, and software
Charting and Education	www.echarts.com	Charting and educational materials
Charting and News	www.barcharts.com	Charting and company information
Technical Analysis of Stocks and Commodities	www.traders.com	Articles related to trading
Active Trader magazine	www.activetradermag.com	Articles related to trading
Futures magazine	www.futuresmag.com	Articles related to trading

Stock and Stock Index Option Symbols

Table B.6 lists all the available options for America Online (symbol: AOL) as of December 28, 2000. Due to stock price splits and large price movements there are three different option root symbols: AOE, AOO, AOL. To place an option order on-line you must use the appropriate root symbol. The best source of this information is the following link via the CBOE: http://quote.cboe .com/quotetable.htm.

1. Go to this link and enter the underlying stock symbol.
2. Click "List all options and LEAPS."
3. Click "Submit."

To download this information, follow Steps 1 and 2 above, then click "Download Text File." Enter the underlying stock symbol again and click "Download."

Stock Option Volume Statistics

Table B.7 gives you some idea of the level of option trading volume among the most actively traded stocks.

Table B.6 America Online Options Available on December 28, 2000

Option Symbol	Expiration Month	Expiration Year	Strike Price	Call/Put	Option Symbol	Expiration Month	Expiration Year	Strike Price	Call/Put
AOL AA	1	1	5	C	AOL MA	1	1	5	P
AOL AY	1	1	5.625	C	AOL MY	1	1	5.625	P
AOL AZ	1	1	6.25	C	AOL MZ	1	1	6.25	P
AOL AE	1	1	6.875	C	AOL ME	1	1	6.875	P
AOL AU	1	1	7.5	C	AOL MU	1	1	7.5	P
AOL AF	1	1	8.125	C	AOL MF	1	1	8.125	P
AOL AG	1	1	8.75	C	AOL MG	1	1	8.75	P
AOL AH	1	1	9.375	C	AOL MH	1	1	9.375	P
AOL AB	1	1	10	C	AOL MB	1	1	10	P
AOL AI	1	1	10.625	C	AOL MI	1	1	10.625	P
AOL AJ	1	1	11.25	C	AOL MJ	1	1	11.25	P
AOL AK	1	1	11.875	C	AOL MK	1	1	11.875	P
AOL AV	1	1	12.5	C	AOL MV	1	1	12.5	P
AOL AL	1	1	13.125	C	AOL ML	1	1	13.125	P
AOL AM	1	1	13.75	C	AOL MM	1	1	13.75	P
AOL AC	1	1	15	C	AOL MC	1	1	15	P
AOL AO	1	1	15.625	C	AOL MO	1	1	15.625	P
AOL AP	1	1	16.25	C	AOL MP	1	1	16.25	P
AOL AQ	1	1	16.875	C	AOL MQ	1	1	16.875	P
AOL AW	1	1	17.5	C	AOL MW	1	1	17.5	P
AOL AR	1	1	18.125	C	AOL MR	1	1	18.125	P
AOL AS	1	1	18.75	C	AOL MS	1	1	18.75	P
AOL AT	1	1	19.375	C	AOL MT	1	1	19.375	P
AOL AD	1	1	20	C	AOL MD	1	1	20	P
AOL BD	2	1	20	C	AOL ND	2	1	20	P
AOL DD	4	1	20	C	AOL PD	4	1	20	P

(continues)

259

Table B.6 America Online Options Available on December 28, 2000 (*Continued*)

Option Symbol	Expiration Month	Expiration Year	Strike Price	Call/Put	Option Symbol	Expiration Month	Expiration Year	Strike Price	Call/Put
AOL GD	7	1	20	C	AOL SD	7	1	20	P
AOL AN	1	1	21.25	C	AOL MN	1	1	21.25	P
AOL AX	1	1	22.5	C	AOL MX	1	1	22.5	P
AOL BX	2	1	22.5	C	AOL NX	2	1	22.5	P
AOL DX	4	1	22.5	C	AOL PX	4	1	22.5	P
AOL GX	7	1	22.5	C	AOL SX	7	1	22.5	P
AOE AK	1	1	23.75	C	AOE MK	1	1	23.75	P
AOE AE	1	1	25	C	AOE ME	1	1	25	P
AOE BE	2	1	25	C	AOE NE	2	1	25	P
AOE DE	4	1	25	C	AOE PE	4	1	25	P
AOE GE	7	1	25	C	AOE SE	7	1	25	P
AOE AL	1	1	26.25	C	AOE ML	1	1	26.25	P
AOE AY	1	1	27.5	C	AOE MY	1	1	27.5	P
AOE BY	2	1	27.5	C	AOE NY	2	1	27.5	P
AOE DY	4	1	27.5	C	AOE PY	4	1	27.5	P
AOE GY	7	1	27.5	C	AOE SY	7	1	27.5	P
AOE AM	1	1	28.75	C	AOE MM	1	1	28.75	P
AOE AF	1	1	30	C	AOE MF	1	1	30	P
AOE BF	2	1	30	C	AOE NF	2	1	30	P
AOE DF	4	1	30	C	AOE PF	4	1	30	P
AOE GF	7	1	30	C	AOE SF	7	1	30	P
AOE AN	1	1	31.25	C	AOE MN	1	1	31.25	P
AOE AZ	1	1	32.5	C	AOE MZ	1	1	32.5	P
AOE BZ	2	1	32.5	C	AOE NZ	2	1	32.5	P
AOE DZ	4	1	32.5	C	AOE PZ	4	1	32.5	P
AOE GZ	7	1	32.5	C	AOE SZ	7	1	32.5	P
AOE AO	1	1	33.75	C	AOE MO	1	1	33.75	P

AOE AG	1	1	35	C
AOE BG	2	1	35	C
AOE DG	4	1	35	C
AOE GG	7	1	35	C
AOE AU	1	1	37.5	C
AOE BU	2	1	37.5	C
AOE DU	4	1	37.5	C
AOE GU	7	1	37.5	C
AOE AH	1	1	40	C
AOE BH	2	1	40	C
AOE DH	4	1	40	C
AOE GH	7	1	40	C
AOE AR	1	1	41.25	C
AOE AV	1	1	42.5	C
AOE BV	2	1	42.5	C
AOE DV	4	1	42.5	C
AOE GV	7	1	42.5	C
AOE AS	1	1	43.75	C
AOE AI	1	1	45	C
AOE BI	2	1	45	C
AOE DI	4	1	45	C
AOE GI	7	1	45	C
AOE AT	1	1	46.25	C
AOE AW	1	1	47.5	C
AOE BW	2	1	47.5	C
AOE DW	4	1	47.5	C
AOE GW	7	1	47.5	C
AOE AX	1	1	48.75	C
AOO AJ	1	1	50	C
AOO BJ	2	1	50	C
AOO DJ	4	1	50	C

AOE MG	1	1	35	P
AOE NG	2	1	35	P
AOE PG	4	1	35	P
AOE SG	7	1	35	P
AOE MU	1	1	37.5	P
AOE NU	2	1	37.5	P
AOE PU	4	1	37.5	P
AOE SU	7	1	37.5	P
AOE MH	1	1	40	P
AOE NH	2	1	40	P
AOE PH	4	1	40	P
AOE SH	7	1	40	P
AOE MR	1	1	41.25	P
AOE MV	1	1	42.5	P
AOE NV	2	1	42.5	P
AOE PV	4	1	42.5	P
AOE SV	7	1	42.5	P
AOE MS	1	1	43.75	P
AOE MI	1	1	45	P
AOE NI	2	1	45	P
AOE PI	4	1	45	P
AOE SI	7	1	45	P
AOE MT	1	1	46.25	P
AOE MW	1	1	47.5	P
AOE NW	2	1	47.5	P
AOE PW	4	1	47.5	P
AOE SW	7	1	47.5	P
AOE MX	1	1	48.75	P
AOO MJ	1	1	50	P
AOO NJ	2	1	50	P
AOO PJ	4	1	50	P

(continues)

Table B.6 America Online Options Available on December 28, 2000 (*Continued*)

Option Symbol	Expiration Month	Expiration Year	Strike Price	Call/Put	Option Symbol	Expiration Month	Expiration Year	Strike Price	Call/Put
AOO GJ	7	1	50	C	AOO SJ	7	1	50	P
AOO AE	1	1	52.5	C	AOO ME	1	1	52.5	P
AOO AK	1	1	55	C	AOO MK	1	1	55	P
AOO BK	2	1	55	C	AOO NK	2	1	55	P
AOO DK	4	1	55	C	AOO PK	4	1	55	P
AOO GK	7	1	55	C	AOO SK	7	1	55	P
AOO AF	1	1	57.5	C	AOO MF	1	1	57.5	P
AOO AL	1	1	60	C	AOO ML	1	1	60	P
AOO BL	2	1	60	C	AOO NL	2	1	60	P
AOO DL	4	1	60	C	AOO PL	4	1	60	P
AOO GL	7	1	60	C	AOO SL	7	1	60	P
AOO AG	1	1	62.5	C	AOO MG	1	1	62.5	P
AOO AM	1	1	65	C	AOO MM	1	1	65	P
AOO BM	2	1	65	C	AOO NM	2	1	65	P
AOO DM	4	1	65	C	AOO PM	4	1	65	P
AOO GM	7	1	65	C	AOO SM	7	1	65	P
AOO AN	1	1	70	C	AOO MN	1	1	70	P
AOO BN	2	1	70	C	AOO NN	2	1	70	P
AOO DN	4	1	70	C	AOO PN	4	1	70	P
AOO GN	7	1	70	C	AOO SN	7	1	70	P
AOO AO	1	1	75	C	AOO MO	1	1	75	P
AOO BO	2	1	75	C	AOO NO	2	1	75	P
AOO DO	4	1	75	C	AOO PO	4	1	75	P
AOO GO	7	1	75	C	AOO SO	7	1	75	P
AOO AW	1	1	77.5	C	AOO MW	1	1	77.5	P
AOO AP	1	1	80	C	AOO MP	1	1	80	P
AOO BP	2	1	80	C	AOO NP	2	1	80	P

AOO DP	4	1	80	C		AOO PP	4	1	80	P
AOO GP	7	1	80	C		AOO SP	7	1	80	P
AOO AX	1	1	82.5	C		AOO MX	1	1	82.5	P
AOO AQ	1	1	85	C		AOO MQ	1	1	85	P
AOO BQ	2	1	85	C		AOO NQ	2	1	85	P
AOO DQ	4	1	85	C		AOO PQ	4	1	85	P
AOO GQ	7	1	85	C		AOO SQ	7	1	85	P
AOO AY	1	1	87.5	C		AOO MY	1	1	87.5	P
AOO AR	1	1	90	C		AOO MR	1	1	90	P
AOO BR	2	1	90	C		AOO NR	2	1	90	P
AOO DR	4	1	90	C		AOO PR	4	1	90	P
AOO GR	7	1	90	C		AOO SR	7	1	90	P
AOO AZ	1	1	92.5	C		AOO MZ	1	1	92.5	P
AOO AS	1	1	95	C		AOO MS	1	1	95	P
AOO AT	1	1	100	C		AOO MT	1	1	100	P
AOO AA	1	1	105	C		AOO MA	1	1	105	P
AOO AB	1	1	110	C		AOO MB	1	1	110	P
AOO AC	1	1	115	C		AOO MC	1	1	115	P
AOO AD	1	1	120	C		AOO MD	1	1	120	P
AOW AE	1	1	125	C		AOW ME	1	1	125	P
AOW AF	1	1	130	C		AOW MF	1	1	130	P
AOW AG	1	1	135	C		AOW MG	1	1	135	P
AOW AH	1	1	140	C		AOW MH	1	1	140	P
AOW AI	1	1	145	C		AOW MI	1	1	145	P

Table B.7 Average Daily Stock Option Volume on CBOE in April 2001

Option Symbol	Stock Symbol	Stock Name	Monthly Volume	Average Daily Volume	Average Daily Call Volume	Average Daily Put Volume
MSQ	MSFT	Microsoft Corporation	1,157,359	57,868	35,453	22,415
CYQ	CSCO	Cisco Systems, Inc.	990,054	49,503	30,012	19,490
EMC	EMC	EMC Corporation	501,173	25,059	14,215	10,844
IBM	IBM	International Business Machines Corporation	485,032	24,252	12,762	11,490
AOL	AOL	AOL Time Warner, Inc.	445,875	22,294	15,810	6484
ORQ	ORCL	Oracle Corporation	407,149	20,357	15,636	4721
GE	GE	General Electric Company	404,377	20,219	12,232	7987
INQ	INTC	Intel Corporation	394,553	19,728	12,003	7725
LU	LU	Lucent Technologies, Inc.	328,996	16,450	12,342	4107
DLQ	DELL	Dell Computer Corp.	328,264	16,413	10,370	6043
JUP	JNPR	Juniper Networks, Inc.	304,835	15,242	6028	9214
C	C	Citigroup, Inc.	299,265	14,963	9176	5787
NOK	NOK	Nokia Corporation ADR	279,137	13,957	10,489	3468
QAQ	QCOM	QUALCOMM, Inc.	265,316	13,266	8118	5148
EUQ	CIEN	Ciena Corporation	260,380	13,019	6260	6759
UQD	JDSU	JDS Uniphase Corp.	249,842	12,492	8573	3919
GLW	GLW	Corning Incorporated	222,847	11,142	7008	4134
NT	NT	Nortel Networks Corporation	220,404	11,020	6702	4319
SUQ	SUNW	Sun Microsystems Inc.	217,373	10,869	8369	2500
TXN	TXN	Texas Instruments Incorporated	217,255	10,863	7580	3,283
UBF	BRCD	Brocade Communications	209,649	10,482	8683	1800
SGQ	SEBL	Siebel Systems, Inc.	202,943	10,147	6,070	4,077
LDQ	WCOM	Worldcom, Inc.	163,137	8157	6157	2000
T	T	AT&T Corporation	156,237	7812	4862	2950
VUQ	VRTS	VERITAS Software Corporation	153,082	7654	3196	4458
YHQ	YHOO	Yahoo! Inc	149,112	7456	4917	2539
MOT	MOT	Motorola, Inc.	140,529	7026	4845	2182
ANQ	AMAT	Applied Materials, Inc.	138,661	6,933	2585	4348
AMD	AMD	Advanced Micro Devices, Inc.	136,242	6,812	4750	2062

INDEX